SO YOU THINK YOU'VE GOT PROBLEMS

TWELVE STUBBORN SAINTS AND THEIR PUSHY PARENTS

Sharon Nastick

Illustrated by James E. McIlrath

Our Sunday Visitor, Inc.
HUNTINGTON • INDIANA

THE MEMORARE

Remember, O most gracious Virgin Mary, that never was it known that anyone who fled to thy protection, implored thy help, or sought thy intercession was left unaided. Inspired by this confidence, I fly unto thee, O Virgin of Virgins, my Mother. To thee do I come. Before thee I stand, sinful and sorrowful. O Mother of the Word Incarnate, despise not my petitions but, in thy mercy, hear and answer me. Amen.

FRANCIS OF SALES
FOUND COMFORT
IN THIS PRAYER.
See page 35.

©1982 by Our Sunday Visitor, Inc.
Huntington, Indiana 46750
All rights reserved

Book designer: Thomas Casaletto

ISBN: 0-87973-661-5
LCCCN: 81-85454

Printed in the USA

CONTENTS

FOREWORD / 1
ST. FRANCES OF ROME / 3
ST. THOMAS AQUINAS / 9
ST. RITA / 22
ST. FRANCIS OF SALES / 30
ST. JOHN CALYBITES / 39
ST. JOAN OF VALOIS / 43
ST. CLARE / 50
ST. MARTIN OF TOURS / 56
ST. ALOYSIUS / 68
ST. ROSE OF VITERBO / 77
ST. WENCESLAUS / 82
ST. CATHERINE OF SIENA / 87
AFTERWORD / 91

"I looked up . . . ."

FOREWORD

When I first sat down to write these saintly sketches, I was filled with high hopes and enthusiasm. I had done all the research. I knew who I wanted to write about and what I wanted to say. I figured I could finish the entire book in a week or two.

But after the first three chapters, my enthusiasm silently stole away. I read over what I had written, and I was not pleased.

"This," I said loudly and clearly, "stinks."

"Agreed," a heavenly voice, or one who claims to possess a heavenly voice, replied.

"But I don't know what's wrong. I've done the research. I have the facts. But something's missing."

"It's the *people* who are missing," the voice claimed as its angelic owner materialized above my desk.

"Nonsense. Look at these names. St. Thomas Aquinas, St. Rita, St. Francis de Sales, St. Jeanne de Valois."

"That's the problem. They're just *names*. They don't come across as people. They lack the personal touch."

"I can't help that," I said sullenly. "I don't know them."

"*I* do."

I looked up to see that smug smile spread across his supposedly cherubic face. Guardian angels ought to be sweet, kind, and patient. I've told Maurice so before. I was about to tell him again but quickly thought of a better idea.

"You know these people?"

"We hang out in the same place, you know."

"Why don't you bring about twelve of your good friends down here so I can talk to them?"

The smug smile sank down into a stern frown. "You know I can't do that. It's against regulations."

"But I need help. You're my guardian angel. You're supposed to help me. How about just one saint? How about St. Thomas Aquinas? I've always wanted to talk to him."

"You'll talk to him one of these days—if you're good." Sometimes Maurice sounds exactly like my third-grade teacher. "In the meantime, you can talk to me."

"Whoopee," I said, not very enthusiastically.

"Oh well, if you don't want my help..." He was starting to dematerialize.

"No! Maurice, wait! I need you! I mean, you can help me if you want to."

He re-solidified. "It's not that *I* want to," he said, "but I have orders from a higher power."

"*Somebody* up there likes me!"

"So what is this book about?"

"It's about twelve saints who had problems with their parents."

"Let's see the names."

I tossed up the list. Maurice suspended it in front of his eyes. "Not bad choices."

"Thank you."

"Where do you want to start?"

"Wherever you like. They're your friends."

"*And* yours," said Maurice as he settled back against an air cushion. "Pick up your pencil. Take notes. I'll ask questions later."

"Great. I just graduated from college, and here I am taking notes again."

"Don't gripe," Maurice ordered. "Write."

So I did. ◈

ST. FRANCES OF ROME

"Well, Maurice, who's on first?"
"Frances."
"Of Assisi?"
"Not Fran*cis*. Fran*ces*. St. Frances of Rome."
"A woman?"
"You object?"
"No! No! I sometimes get those names mixed up. Especially when you pronounce them exactly alike."
"I'm pronouncing them right. You're hearing them wrong."
"Well, pardon *me!*"
"Touchy today, aren't we?"
"*We* certainly are, Maurice, and I wish you would begin before *we* get any touchier.
"Gladly."

"St. Frances was born in Rome in 1384. Her parents were Paul de Buxo and Jacobella Rofredeschi, both members of illustrious and wealthy families."
"I get the picture: Frances was spoiled rotten."
"She could have been, if she hadn't discovered God while she was still a toddler. She soon dedicated her young life to prayer and solitude. She didn't care for children's games or other children's company. She didn't care much for adult company either. God was enough for her."
"Maurice, you sound as though every human being should go off into solitary confinement and ignore everyone else on earth."
"I don't say that. But I think everyone should spend a certain amount of time away from earthly companions."
"But shouldn't we be able to hear the voice of God in every creature?"

By the time Frances was eleven, she was ready to enter a convent.

"But do we? And how do we know God's voice in other creatures unless we first hear God's voice speaking solo?"

"Why can't you let a human win?"

"Keep trying. You may score someday.

"By the time Frances was eleven, she was ready to enter a convent and dedicate her life totally to God. But her parents had other ideas. They had made a splendid match for their child: a rich young nobleman from Rome, Lorenzo Ponziano. They were not about to allow their lovely girl to waste away in a convent, unseen by the world. They wanted her to bloom where everyone could see her.

"When Frances realized that her parents could not be dissuaded, she consented to the wedding, trusting that God's will would be done."

"She was married at *eleven*?"

"At twelve."

"It must have killed them to wait a whole year."

"Don't ask *me* why they moved so fast. I don't understand why humans get married straight out of high school, much less why they used to get married before puberty. But that was how it was in Italy in the fourteenth century. No one thought it odd.

"Frances became quite ill soon after the wedding—"

"No wonder."

"—but she soon recovered and resigned herself to the joys and tribulations of married life."

"At *twelve*?!"

"There's more to marriage than your little mind is presently considering. Frances was mature for her age, mature in homely matters as well as in the grace of God. And her husband was every bit as kind, intelligent, and affectionate as her parents thought he was. They lived together for forty years and never so much as uttered an angry word to each other."

"Maybe more people should marry before junior high."

"It's not the age for that now. Why grow up before you have to?"

"Why, thank you, Maurice! That's what I always say."

"Who do you think said it first?"

"Oh, don't give me that!"

"Relax. It wasn't me. But it wasn't you either."

"Who was it then?"

"Would you like a chronological list of all the people who've said it over the centuries?"

"Skip it, Mo."

"Despite the demands of marriage, including the homemaking and the child rearing that were soon to follow, Frances clung to her old life as tightly as she could. She spent much time in solitude, meditation, prayer, and good works. But she was always available when her husband or her three children needed her for matters great or small. As she once said, 'A married woman must, when called upon, quit her devotion to God at the altar to find Him in her household affairs.' "

"In other words, you can find God at the kitchen sink as well as in church."

"Mm. Let's say, rather, that you can find God in service to others as well as in private prayer. I'd hate to see people substituting household chores for Mass."

"I wouldn't worry too much about that, Angel Guardian. No person in her right mind would rather clean the bathroom than go to church."

"In addition to her rigorous prayer life, Frances imposed high standards on her secular life as well. She abstained from wine, fish, and meat for months at a time, living on sparse amounts of bread and water. Her clothes were made of rough serge, not the fashionable fabrics customary for a lady of her rank. She often wore a hair shirt and a girdle made of horsehair."

"Makes me itch just to think of it. Why'd she do those things?"

"To bring herself closer to God through penance and self-discipline."

"And did it work?"

"Of course. So inspiring was her example that many Roman ladies imitated her. They got together and put themselves under the spiritual direction of the Benedictine monks of Monte-Oliveto. They didn't leave their families, make binding vows, or wear a particular habit, but they lived the holiest lives they could."

"And their husbands didn't object?"

"Most of them didn't."

"Must have been an enlightened age."

"Not as enlightened as you might think. This was not a time of peace but a time of many wars, especially in Italy. Louis of Anjou and Ladislaus were fighting it out for the right to take charge of the kingdom of Naples. In 1398, Ladislaus conquered Rome. While he went on to bigger and better concerns, he appointed Troja, a nasty old soldier, to take charge of the city. Though Troja did not much care for the Roman nobles, he really hated the ones who were still loyal to the Pope. Lorenzo Ponziano was high on his hate list. Troja was quite pleased when some of his soldiers came upon Lorenzo one night and attacked him."

"And killed him?"

"Very nearly. He was swiftly carried home by his friends, and Frances managed to nurse him back to health. Shortly after this incident, Troja noticed that his popularity was slipping. Before he left Rome, he decided to further torment the Ponziani."

"Isn't the family name Ponziano?"

"Yes. But I'm using the Italian plural because I'm talking about more than one family unit."

"You mean he went after all the brothers and the sisters and the cousins and the aunts?"

"Yes. He arrested Paluzzo, Frances's brother, and locked him up. Then he demanded Frances's oldest son, John Baptista, as a hostage."

"How old was John Baptista?"

"Eight or nine."

"Bet she put up a fight."

"What good would fighting have done, except to get them in even more trouble?"

"She didn't just give him up!?"

"Yes she did. She walked through the crowd at the capitol and delivered her son to Troja. Then she ran to the church of Ara Coeli, knelt in the chapel of the Mother of Mercy, and prayed as she had never prayed before.

"Baptista, meanwhile, wasn't sure what was happening to him. But he shared his mother's deep faith, and he wasn't really frightened.

"The crowd in front of the capitol was turning downright rebellious. Troja decided the time had come to make his getaway. He ordered one of his officers to take Baptista onto his horse.

"The moment Baptista was set on its back, the horse stood stock still. No amount of pushing, prodding, cursing, or whipping could make the animal move."

"God turned him into a mule?"

"Not in body but in spirit. And not only this horse but every other horse Baptista was transferred to. The animals might have been made of stone for all the obedience they showed the soldiers.

"Troja was more frightened by this 'coincidence' than he cared to admit. He tried to conceal his terror by gruffly ordering that Baptista be returned to his mother. So the little boy was joyfully carried off to Ara Coeli and restored to Frances's loving arms."

"And that was that."

"But not for long. Ladislaus invaded Rome again in 1410. Lorenzo was obliged to flee for his life, leaving his wife and children behind. They remained in their comfortable home, alone and defenseless.

"Day by day the conquerors came closer and closer to the Ponziano estate. Frances heard reports of their progress: peasants massacred, crops burned, cattle killed. She was utterly surrounded. She knew she could do nothing but wait.

"All too soon they reached her doors. They wrecked the place, disrupting every room, and ended by carrying off Baptista when they left. But Frances and her younger children escaped harm. For the moment, they were safe."

"What happened to Baptista? Was he held hostage again?"

"No. He soon got away from his captors and fled to his father forthwith."

"Fantastic."

"But nothing was fantastic back at Rome. Frances, Evangelista, and Agnese were living in the least damaged room of the house. They were practically without food, clothing, and money. Yet Frances's spirit remained unquenchable. She shared what few goods they had with people who were even more wretched than they. With her sister-in-law's help, she established a makeshift hospital on the lower floor of her ruined palace and cared for the sick who came or were brought there.

"Patients soon arrived in alarming numbers. Famine broke out over the land and was swiftly followed by that most infamous disease, the Black Death. Evangelista and Agnese were among its victims. Frances herself became quite ill, but she slowly recovered.

"In 1414, Ladislaus died. Peace returned to Italy. Lorenzo and the other Ponziani who had fled the country returned home and found their property and dignity fully restored to them.

"Lorenzo came home an old and broken man. Frances, too, was much changed. But their love was as strong as—nay, stronger than ever before. She devoted herself unsparingly to him, caring for him through the illness that was to be his last.

"Soon after his return to Rome, Lorenzo gave his wife permission to live as she pleased, with his blessing. When she had a spare moment, she set about realizing one of her fondest dreams. It came partially true in 1425, when she founded the Oblate Order of nuns. She joined them and became their superior when her husband died in 1436."

"She waited a long time."

"Forty years."

"And three children."

"And a lot of pain and suffering."

"You don't always paint a very rosy picture of sainthood, Maurice."

"Roses have thorns," Maurice observed cryptically before fading out for the day.

ST. THOMAS AQUINAS

"Good morning," I caroled as soon as the first golden fragments of Maurice appeared.

"*You're* up early," Maurice said grumpily with as much as had formed of his voice.

"Why aren't you?"

"I had a tough time getting through this atmosphere of yours. Pollution so thick a mortal could walk on it! Don't you know what you're doing to your sole supply of air with all your factories and automobiles?"

"Sure we know, Maurice. We're just not doing anything about it."

"Well, you *should*," he snapped, flapping dust and dirt off of his wings and onto my desk, "before it's too late."

I chased away the smog with a wave of my hand. "I'll write the President a letter. Right now I want to hear about St. Thomas Aquinas."

Maurice's glower vanished in an understanding glow. "That's why the bright morning face, eh?"

"You bet! I've been waiting for this for a good long time."

"You like Thomas?"

"Oh sure, Maurice, I've always liked Thomas. I'm really keen on his early trials and tribulations. Not many future saints get locked up in the family castle for not doing what Mommy wanted them to do."

Maurice grinned. "You've done your homework, I see."

"It wasn't hard to do. A lot has been written about Thomas. But I'd still appreciate your personal touch."

My guardian angel forgot about the messy air and the smudges on the hem of his robe. He leaned against the bookcase and clasped both hands around one knee. "Get out a clean sheet of paper—make sure you have plenty, by the way, because this is a long one—and I'll begin.

"But before I start to tell Thomas's story, you should know something about Thomas's family. In their way, they are quite as remarkable as Thomas himself."

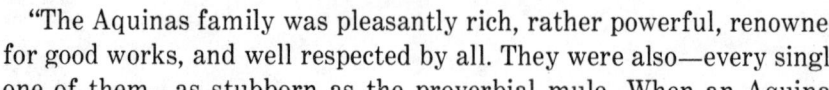

"The Aquinas family was pleasantly rich, rather powerful, renowned for good works, and well respected by all. They were also—every single one of them—as stubborn as the proverbial mule. When an Aquinas mind was made up, it stayed made up, come hell, high water, or anything short of divine intervention.

"At the time of Thomas's birth, the heads of this royal family were Landulf, count of Aquinas, and Theodora of Theate. They already had six children, two boys and four girls, but the arrival of the third son was celebrated by everyone in the house. All had prayed for a boy, but I don't think even Theodora realized what a son God had given them.

"Prior to Thomas's birth, Landulf and Theodora had neatly planned out their newborn's life. Their older boys, Landulf and Reynaldo, had entered the army of Frederick II, as had their father before them. But this boy they would give to the service of the Church."

"Whether he wanted to go or not?"

"He would want to go."

"But he might not want to give up the family money and prestige and all the other good stuff."

"If he let his parents work things out for him, he wouldn't have to. An Aquinas was not going to become a country prelate or a ragged contemplative. Thomas, his parents had decided, was to become the lord abbot of Monte Cassino, a rich and powerful position that would insure both steady income and personal prestige. As an added convenience, the abbey wasn't very far from home."

"Where is home, by the way?"

"The family castle stood at Rocca Secca, Italy, not far from Naples.

"Thomas was born sometime early in the year 1225 and lived a happy life at home until he was five years old. Then his mother packed his schoolbag and sent him off to become an oblate in the monastery his parents planned to give him."

"Hold it a second, Maruice. How can his parents *give* him a monastery? Do they own it?"

"Not exactly. They didn't own the property or the monks, but they shared mutual interests. The monastery and the Aquinas family, in fact, hadn't always been on good terms with each other. In 1229, a year before Thomas first entered those holy gates, Frederick's troops had ravaged the abbey. Landulf had led the charge. No one was was killed, but property and crops were destroyed. The lord abbot was eloquently angry."

"Why didn't Landulf refuse to attack the monastery?"

"Because, despite his health and power, Landulf was under the orders of Frederick II, and it is not wise to disobey your emperor, no matter who you are."

"I'll keep that in mind."

"After that incident, Landulf realized that he had offended the men who were to play a most important part in his son's life and that it would be prudent to make up with them as soon as possible. In time they worked out a mutually satisfactory arrangement involving money and protection and other worldly matters."

"Good enough, Maurice. Now, about Thomas, isn't a boy of five a little young to be sent to live with a bunch of solemn old men?"

"Come on, it wasn't as bad as all that. There were a few young monks. But youth and age weren't of special interest to Thomas. As long as he had books and teachers, he was content."

"Did he always love books?"

"From his infancy, practically. He was a born scholar. 'Just like me,' you're thinking, but you're not quite conceited enough to say it."

"You said it, Mr. Guardian Angel, I didn't."

"Thomas proved to be an almost perfect student: obedient, respectful, diligent in his duties and studies, pious in prayer. But he did have an annoying habit, one that caused his teachers considerable distress. He constantly asked, 'What is God?' And no matter how many answers he received, he wasn't satisified. He drove the monks nearly mad with his one-track mind.

"Thomas stayed at the monastery for about nine years, until he was fourteen. By then he had learned all that the monks could teach him, and he was ready to go on to bigger and better things. His father arranged his transfer to the University of Naples."

"He never got too far from home."

"He never needed to. Everything he needed was within reach by foot or horse.

"Naples was something of a shock to the boy from rural Italy. By that era's standards, Naples was a large city, twice the size of any town Thomas had ever seen, and twice as bad as anything Thomas had ever imagined. The traditional student life of wine, women, and song was in full swing, and available to everyone.

"Theodora knew what Naples was like. She was not about to allow her youngest child to become contaminated by earthly desires. She arranged for him to lodge at one of the Benedictine houses in the city, where he could live a private life like the one he had known at Monte Cassino."

"Ho-hum."

"Thomas wasn't unhappy there. Remember, he was only fourteen and not awfully interested in the three things I just mentioned. Thomas soon showed his new teachers that his scholastic reputation had been well earned. They spoke glowingly of his brilliant future. The young count would certainly succeed at whatever he put his mind to.

"But though he was satisfied with his studies, Thomas wasn't confortable with the Benedictines. He admired their spirituality, but he didn't care for their involvement in earthly matters. He wanted a simpler life, a life that would give him time to read, study, think, and write; time to pursue the answer to his favorite question, *What is God?*

"While he was in Naples, he discovered the Dominicans. They could offer him the life he wanted: the combination of learning and holiness, and with a minimum of outside distractions. When he was seventeen years old, he applied for admission to the Order."

"Welcomed with open arms, I suppose?"

"Not exactly. The prior, Thomas Agni de Lentino, advised him to consider his vocation for a year or two before he finally made up his mind."

"Because Thomas was only seventeen?"

"Partly that. And partly because the prior wished to avoid tangling with the Aquinas family. After all, a Dominican was not what Thomas was supposed to be. There was no money and no prestige in teaching."

"Guess some things never change."

"During that year, Thomas told his parents what he wanted to do. They did not react well to the news. Landulf threatened the Dominicans with all the nasty things he could think of, but the friars refused to be bullied into submission. If Thomas sincerely wanted to join them, he would be welcome. If not, that was fine too.

"When he couldn't convince the Dominicans, Landulf argued with his son. Thomas listened patiently, considered his father's point of view, then explained again why he wished to become a Dominican. The stalemate lasted for a long time, but before his death in 1243, Landulf gave Thomas his consent.

"After mourning for his father, Thomas returned to Naples and Agni de Lentino. This time he was accepted and welcomed into the monastery. After the requisite year of training, he was formally received into the Dominican Order of Preachers in 1244, trading all his worldly riches for a simple white habit and a life of poverty."

"Hold on a minute, Maurice. You said that Landulf gave his consent to his son's vocation. But I'll bet Theodora didn't give up so easily."

"For a long time—the year Thomas was in training—she didn't know what was going on. She assumed her son was continuing his work at the university."

"Did he tell a lie?"

'No. He just told her, 'I'm going back to Naples, Mother,' and left."

"Man of few words."

"Never was much of a talker. He knew word was likely to reach Rocca Secca after his ordination to the priesthood, so he suggested to his superiors that he be sent out of Italy as soon as possible. Agni de Lentino didn't have to ask why. He immediately made arrangements for a trip to Rome."

"That's not out of Italy."

"No, but it's on the way out of Italy. They couldn't just 'hop a plane,' you know. The plan was to keep Thomas in Rome until Theodora was looking in another direction, then smuggle him into Germany. Theodora found out and she was enraged. As though she didn't have enough trouble with settling her late husband's affairs and interviewing prospective husbands for her daughters, now her youngest son had to go and place his future in jeopardy. Obviously he had to be saved from himself. She took off for Naples at once. But by the time she got there, Thomas was well on his way to Rome."

"Hooray!"

"Theodora stayed in Naples just long enough to tell the Dominicans exactly what she thought of them."

"Tsk tsk."

"Then she hurried to Rome, where she landed on the doorstep of Santa Sabina, the most prominent Dominican house. When she demanded to see her son, she was told that her son did not wish to see her."

"That probably wasn't too smart."

"A debatable point. In any case, Theodora was temporarily stalled. She took rooms in a respectable inn while she figured out what to do next.

"Meanwhile, the Dominicans finalized their own plot: They would move Thomas to Cologne, in what is now West Germany, as quickly and quietly as possible. But while they gathered up food and horses, they unwittingly gave Theodora exactly what she needed: time—time to get in touch with her older sons and tell them what she wanted done.

"Landulf and Reynaldo, you may recall, were soldiers—officers, I should say—in the emperor's army. They were able to put all roads out of Rome under constant watch. Any monks, Dominican monks in particular, were to be stopped and searched."

"And Thomas and his friends walked right into the trap."

"You *have* done your homework."

"I told you I liked this story, Maurice."

"Anything involving royalty and castles gets your attention."

"It's a Leo characteristic."

"Don't get me started on astrology. As you said, Thomas and his friends walked into the arms of his brothers. With some difficulty, Thomas was separated from his friends and dragged off to Rocca Secca, where his mother awaited him."

"With sharpened claws and treacherous tongue."

"Yes. She had spent a lot of anger on other people, but she stil had some left over for her son. She reminded Thomas of his duty to the family. Their fortunes were not stable, she said. If he did what he was supposed to do, if he became the lord abbot at Monte Cassino, all their problems would be solved. He would still have a priestly vocation, and his family wouldn't have to worry about where the money was coming from. He would also make his widowed mother very happy."

"Oh brother."

"Thomas heard her out, then carefully, rationally, argued against her plan. He did not wish to be abbot. More important, he did not feel that God wanted him to be an abbot. He wanted to study questions of great importance, especially his favorite one. He wanted to teach. His brothers and sisters could look after the other things. Despite his mother's gloomy predictions, the family was far from being in danger of starvation or ruin. One child surely could be spared from secular concerns. He, Thomas, was the obvious choice.

"Since her attempts to argue Thomas into compliance hadn't worked, Theodora next turned to tears and lamentations. He was breaking his mother's heart with his selfish stubbornness, sending her to an early grave. Was she asking for so much? Had she ever asked anything of him before? How—how—how could he be so heartless? Et cetera.

"Thomas's heart was touched, but he forced himself to stand firm. When she paused to dry her face, he calmly explained his position once more.

"Having exhausted her appeals to reason and to emotion without success, Theodora fell back on her final weapon: personal power. Thomas obviously needed time to think, to reconsider his position. She would gladly keep him at home until he decided to do the right thing. She would do this even if he didn't agree to go along with her plan.

"Thereupon Thomas was conducted to the Tower of San Gioranni, a secluded part of the family castle, where he was detained under lock and key for the next year."

St. Thomas Aquinas

"How romantic!"

"Don't go dreamy-eyed, young one. It wasn't as romantic as all that. He wasn't chained to a dungeon wall or fed bread and water once a week. Despite his mother's displeasure, despite the grief he had caused his family, he was still an Aquinas and deserved to be treated as one. His rooms were comfortably furnished, the view from the windows pleasant, the meals regular and plentiful. Two things were denied him: his books and his Dominican friends."

"The two things he loved most."

"Two things he loved much."

"So he wasn't really happy there."

"No. But he endured his captivity with his usual patience and good grace."

"And stubbornness."

"And stubbornness," Maurice granted with a grin. "The only human beings he saw during his first few months in the tower were his sisters, Theodora and Marietta. They seasoned his meals with naggings, pleadings, and lamentations on his mother's favorite theme: *Get thee to the right monastery!*

"But Thomas was more than a match for any arguments his sisters could present. And his sisters weren't as mad at him as his mother was. They loved their big, strong 'baby brother' and felt some sympathy for his plight, as they had known Theodora's wrath before. Thus they soon were converted to his cause."

"Did Theodora find out?"

"Not right away.

"With his sisters on his side, Thomas found that his life was becoming less unpleasant. With their help, he was able to contact his Dominican brethren in Naples. As they couldn't come in person, they sent him cheerful messages, words of encouragement, promises of prayers, and—ah!—books. The Bible, the *Sentences* of Peter Lombard, and some works of the Greek philosopher Aristotle gave Thomas something to do with the quiet hours of the day.

"In good time he had other companions besides his books and his sisters. Imagine his surprise and delight when those remarkable young ladies managed to smuggle Father John of Saint Julian in to see him."

"Wow! Er ... umm ... who's he?"

"Only the most famous Dominican preacher in Italy—perhaps in all the world. Thomas had admired him from afar for a long time. Their meeting, despite the unusual circumstances, was a joyful one. And it wasn't the only meeting they ever had. Father John returned as often as he could. In addition to spiritual advice and hours of good conversation, he brought Thomas some badly needed clothes."

"I thought you said Theodora gave him everything he needed."

"She did. But when Thomas refused to shed his Dominican habit, she swore that he would live in it until he decided to don a Benedictine habit or civilian wear. By the time Father John arrived, his robe had become rather frayed around the edges."

"More holey than holy, eh?"

"I'll let that pass."

"For the next month or two, the tower of San Gioranni, despite being Thomas's prison, was an altogether nice place to visit. The four conspirators spent many happy hours together, talking of God and all things good."

"But it didn't last."

"How do you know?"

"I did my homework, Maurice. Besides, happiness is inevitably attacked by sorrow."

"Forgive me, child of the twentieth century, if I don't share your unduly pessimistic view of the world. I won't argue with you this time, however, because this time you're right. Landulf and Reynaldo, Thomas's soldier brothers, returned home for a surprise visit and found all sorts of surprises awaiting them. First they found Father John on his way home. Since he was trespassing on their property, they promptly tossed him into the family jail."

"Men of action."

"As soon as he was taken care of, the two brothers dashed up the winding tower stairs and burst into Thomas's room."

"Without knocking?"

"Without knocking."

"*Rude* men of action."

"They found him studying the books he wasn't supposed to have and wearing the new habit Father John had just brought him. Thomas greeted them cordially. I regret to report that his brothers weren't nearly so polite."

"Tsk, tsk."

"It didn't take long for his brothers to figure out that their sisters were responsible for these 'outrages.' They reported their findings to their mother—"

"*Tattled* is the word."

"—who was perfectly willing to dismiss her daughters from their duties as jailers and appoint her sons to replace them."

"Didn't the army object?"

"No. The army was stationed nearby and not doing much, so the boys had plenty of free time on their hands.

"Unfortunately for Thomas."

"Also unfortunately for Thomas, his brothers weren't nearly as nice as his sisters. They didn't just talk; they acted. They planned to mix business with pleasure: change their brother's mind and have a little fun at the same time.

"The Tower of San Gioranni, once as quiet and peaceful as a college classroom, now became a popular clubroom for the most riotous section of the army. The older sons of Aquinas and their friends indulged in drinking, singing songs of military life, and outdoing each other with stories of conquests—both on and off the battlefield."

"Must've been hard to concentrate on holy matters. Kind of like having the stereo, radio, and TV on full blast and trying to do your homework."

"Since Thomas couldn't escape from the racket, or the nasty comments that came his way, he had no choice but to ignore them. He withdrew into the farthest corner and kept to himself. He stared out of the window and meditated. I should mention that his brothers had confiscated all his books, though they did allow him to keep his robe."

"Nice guys."

"Even sitting in the corner, Thomas managed to discourage some of the cruder revelry. More and more of the soldiers began to drop off after a few weeks. Whether they were ashamed of teasing a man with such good intentions or because they were tired of the castle, I leave you to judge."

"So Thomas wins the first round."

"Landulf and Reynaldo held a hasty council of war. It didn't take long for them to come up with a better idea. If men couldn't get to Thomas, maybe—just maybe—a woman could."

"You mean they wanted to find a . . ."

"Hush your mouth" said Maurice. "Let's just say they needed a woman who could be bought."

"That sounds even worse than what I was going to say."

"Landulf and Reynaldo went to Naples and, after diligent searching—"

"Nothing was too much work, no pain too great to take, for their dear, dear brother."

"—discovered a fair young beauty and arranged for her to sneak into their home."

"Payment in advance?"

"Of course. She wasn't dumb. As far as the Aquinas boys could see, if anyone could corrupt their brother, she could."

"Did Theodora know what was going on?"

"No. But she may not have forbidden it if she had. Thomas had been locked up for almost a year now without giving in, and her patience was wearing thin."

"Even Aquinases have their limits."

"Yes. And unfortunately for our Naples beauty, Theodora wasn't the only one who was nearing the end of the rope.

"When the young lady first appeared at his chamber door, Thomas welcomed her with his customary politeness. He assumed she was a friend of his sisters. But pretty soon he realized that she hadn't come to talk."

"How far did she get?"

"Not very. She hadn't even shed her shoes. When Thomas saw what she was up to, his temper finally broke. With astounding speed for such a large fellow, he seized a burning brand from the fireplace and chased her out of the room with it."

"Bet she ran all the way back to Naples!"

"And a little farther. When she was gone, Thomas used the red-hot brand to burn a cross into his door. Then, his anger already extinguished, he closed the door and quietly returned to his interrupted business.

"His brothers had witnessed all this from a doorway in the hall. They were too frightened to do anything but watch."

"I don't blame them."

"After their fear wore off, they knew that they still had a problem. Nothing had worked to change Thomas's mind. They had to think of something else, and soon."

"What was left?"

"I'm sure I don't know," Maurice said drily. "They seem to have exhausted every possibility. But before they could hit upon a new plan, help came from an unexpected source."

"The cavalry came over the hill?"

"You could say that. Theodora had tried to keep her son's imprisonment a secret. But news travels fast, and secret news travels faster. Soon after the incident involving the 'lady' from Naples, word of Thomas's plight reached the ears of the Pope himself."

"It took a year to reach his ears?"

"News didn't travel *quite* as fast then as it does now," Maurice conceded, "but it didn't take a year for the Pope to reply. He quickly sent Theodora a message expressing his indignation and hinting that if Thomas were not set free at once, the entire Aquinas family would be excommunicated, wealth and power notwithstanding."

"He *was* upset."

"Theodora knew a threat when she heard it. But she wasn't about to open the door to let Thomas walk out. That would be admitting defeat, and the Aquinas family did not admit defeat. Instead, she arranged for his escape by dropping a few strong hints to her daughters, who were happy to help out.

"So, on a pleasant evening in the summer of 1245, the future saint was lowered from his window via rope and a very large wicker basket to his Dominican brethren waiting below."

"A question, Guardian Angel: Why hadn't Thomas tried to escape before?"

"He never had the means to do it. No ropes, no baskets, not enough sheets on his bed to make a ladder. And his door was always locked. After he had converted his sisters, he didn't feel it was fair to betray their trust by deserting them. And after his brothers came home, he was totally trapped."

"I see. But at last he was safe and free."

"Not quite. While he was being lowered down the tower wall, Theodora was drafting a letter to Innocent IV, the Pope I mentioned earlier, wherein she informed him that she had consented to his wishes like the dutiful daughter of the Church she was. She also asked him to annul her son's Domincan vows on the ground that he had been tricked into taking them."

"That woman never gives up, does she?"

"Have patience. We're almost at the end.

"Innocent was growing weary of this conflict. He had more important things to do than referee family quarrels. The only way to be done with Theodora, he decided, was to settle this matter for once and for all. He already knew Theodora's side. Now he summoned Thomas to Rome to speak on his own behalf.

"Thomas came. And he spoke. In fact, this time he spoke as well as he wrote, which didn't always happen. He told Innocent that no one had tricked him into the Domincan Order; he had wanted to enter it, and he had. But he couldn't blame his family for the way they had treated him. He knew they were disappointed that he hadn't followed his parents' plan. He was sorry that his conscience would not let him do what they wanted him to do.

Thomas was lowered from his window in a very large wicker basket.

St. Thomas Aquinas

"Innocent heard him out, then suggested a compromise. He offered to make Thomas head of Monte Cassino, as his mother wished, while allowing him to retain his Dominican calling rather than switch to the Benedictine life-style."

"Could Innocent do that, Maurice?"

"Of course he could. He was Pope. But Thomas politely turned down the offer. He explained again that he didn't want a public position. He wanted only to pursue his studies in peace.

"Innocent returned a judgment in his favor. As they used to say, '*Roma locuta est; causa finita.*'"*

"In other words, no more arguments."

"The Aquinas family finally had to surrender."

"Did they ever speak to their black-sheep son again?"

"They forgave him, finally. His sisters did better than that: they imitated his good example. Marietta became a nun. Theodora married and lived a truly noble life of kindness and service to others."

"So love of God once again conquers all."

"Combined with faith and sheer determination."

"*Bullheadedness* is the word."

"I prefer *stubbornness*," Maurice said. But his grin suggested that he thought my word an equally apt description. ◈

Rome has spoken; the case is closed.

ST. RITA

"You're late," I said to Maurice the second he materialized.

"I'm sorry. I had more important business to attend to."

"Such as what?"

"Never mind," he said as he made himself comfortable on a soft stretch of air. "It's not mortal business."

"Hmmph," said I, not knowing what else to say.

"But now I am prepared to descend to mortal business."

"It's not too far to go," I reminded Maurice. "It has been said that man is only a little lower than the angels."

"That," Maurice reminded me, "was said by man, not by the angels. But shall we get on with the saint of the day? Who is it?"

"St. Rita."

"Your enthusiasm is heartening."

"It's just that I think I can write this story with no research at all."

"Try."

"Okay. God-fearing girl wishes to enter convent. Parents promptly marry her off to a nice young man. After a happy marriage and several lovely children, the husband dies and the widow is free to pursue her original vocation."

"Wrong."

"Wrong?"

"St. Rita's story encompasses both miracles and agony, joy and heartbreak, all bound together by incredible faith and love of God."

"This sounds interesting."

"It is. Especially as you humans take such interest in stories of human torment and suffering."

"Because those are things we all experience. Everyone but angels, that is."

St. Rita

"Hmmph," Maurice said, which is what he always says when I'm right.

"So tell me about St. Rita."

"All right. But don't turn her story into a soap opera!"

"I won't," I promised.

"The story doesn't begin with St. Rita. It begins with her parents."

"Most of our stories do."

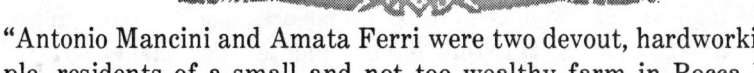

"Antonio Mancini and Amata Ferri were two devout, hardworking people, residents of a small and not too wealthy farm in Rocca Porena, Spain. Neither rich nor poor, they were almost as comfortable as they could hope to be. Their only grief was that they had no children."

"Nowadays people are grieved if they *do* have children."

"Not *all* people."

"*Seems* like all people."

"*Seems* isn't *is*," Maurice said pointedly.

"Another memorable quote."

"Husband and wife prayed for a child for a long time, but when Amata passed her fiftieth birthday, they gave up. Shortly thereafter, Amata became pregnant."

"Why does God always do that?"

"Do what?"

"Answer your prayers after you've given up on them."

"To teach you not to give up on them—among other reasons.

"Amata and Antonio were amazed beyond all telling and happy beyond all description. They counted the days until the child was due. They fixed up a corner of the cottage for the child, sewed clothes, and prepared with all their might for the greatest joy of their lives.

"The child was born on the twenty-second day of May, 1381. Her parents named her Rita. From the day of her birth, Rita proved to be a remarkable child, perhaps because she had been prayed for so long and desired so much. There are many stories of early miracles. My favorite is the story of the white bees."

"White bees? I've never seen white bees."

"Aren't likely to either, unless you go to Spain. When Rita was five days old, a swarm of white bees—the first ever seen on your planet—appeared out of nowhere and flew in and out of her mouth without harming her."

"Yuck."

"You sound like her parents," Maurice chided. "I can assure you that Rita thought it was great fun. The white bees, now known as St. Rita's bees, can still be found in Spain and in other parts of Europe. They lingered near her—outside her various homes—throughout her life."

"The white bees are still around?"

"Yes."

"Could I see one?"

"I suppose so."

With a fancy twist of his hand and a flinging back of his sleeve, Maurice made a fist and opened it. A bee hovered over his palm. It was totally white from antenna to tail, and not uncute, as bees go.

"Pretty neat," I admitted. "But I don't think I'd want a dozen of them swarming all over me."

"Tastes differ," Maurice observed drily as he closed his fist around the bee and made it disappear.

"I guess her parents were pretty impressed."

"And they were scared too. But the wonders decreased as Rita grew up. From a sweet baby, she became a pious child, a perfect daughter, from the parental point of view. She helped her aging parents around the house and farm, went to school and got good grades, never did anything to worry them or make them unhappy. Whenever she had a moment to herself, she prayed.

"By the time she was twelve years old, Rita knew exactly what she wanted to be when she grew up. She asked her parents for permission to leave home and enter the convent at Cascia, not many miles away.

"Observe the peculiarity of earthly parents. Antonio and Amata had prayed countless years for a child. When that child was given to them, they saw miracles happening all around her. They must have known that Rita would belong to God in a very special way. But when Rita asked for this favor—the first she had ever asked for in all her life—they were aghast. How could she want to leave them? And at such a young age too! What had they ever done to her to make her want to escape their home?

"Useless it was for Rita to explain that she loved her parents and did not wish to abandon them, but that the love of God called her to a new life in His serivce. Her parents were too upset to listen. She could calm them only by promising to postpone her journey for a little while.

"As soon as they were sure that Rita wouldn't dash off to Cascia the moment their backs were turned, Antonio and Amata relaxed for a while. But soon they began to think again. If Rita did enter the convent, there would be no grandchildren to treasure, no son-in-law to look after Rita and, in time, take over the family farm. No, Rita did not know what was best for her, but her parents did, and they would take care of her, quickly, before she could think more about going to a convent."

St. Rita

"Maurice, why do parents always think they know what's best?"

"Sometimes they do."

"Most of the time they don't."

"It probably comes down to half and half," Maurice said after thinking a moment, "with parents having the slightly larger half."

"I suppose Rita's parents married her off to the first Catholic bachelor they found?"

"Not exactly. They conducted a long search for the right man. They loved Rita very much, you know. They wanted to marry her to a good man, and they thought they found him in Ferdinand. He was handsome, dashing, and had money and property. They couldn't possibly do better."

"And so they were married."

"And so they were married."

"And lived happily together until the good Ferdinand died."

"Er . . . no. Not exactly."

I looked up from the paper. "Is this where the heartbreak and sorrow come in?"

"Yes."

"Finally! Oops . . . ! I mean, I'm sorry to hear that. Go on."

Maurice moaned in an I-told-you-so fashion but went on with the story.

"Ferdinand was indeed handsome, dashing, and all the rest of it. But he was also haughty, proud, and used to getting his own way. He was leading a dissolute sort of life, and he saw no reason to change his habits just because he was getting married.

"Rita's parents saw none of his faults. They saw only the polished surface and didn't think to look at the heart. And Rita, after much distress and prayer, conceded that God's will might be worked out through the will of her parents. So she consented to the marriage as cheerfully as she could.

"When Ferndinand's true nature emerged after the marriage, it was too late to do anything about it."

"They couldn't arrange an annulment?"

"Not in those days. It's not easy now, and it was nearly impossible then. An annulment was a scandal, and no one wanted a scandal."

"So Rita, I take it, was left to her husband's mercy, or lack of it."

"Literally true. He ruled over her with an iron hand, struck her often. She couldn't even go out to church without his permission."

"And she endured all this?"

"She did. She obeyed her husband's commands, accepted his treatment without giving tit for tat, and prayed for him continually."

"I would have slugged him back, knocked him cold, and left him."

"That's why Rita is a saint and you're not," Maurice replied softly.

"If suffering in silence is all one has to do to become a saint . . ."

"Think a moment. How many people suffer in silence?"

"Your point, Maurice. Let's get back to the marriage."

"In due course of time, Rita gave birth to two sons, Gian Giacomo and Paolo. She tried to raise them as she herself had been raised, instilled with a deep love of God and devotion to parents. But rather than follow her gentle example, her sons chose to emulate their father."

"Bummer! And all this time she was praying."

"Praying, and working hard, and living a remarkable life, setting a stunning example of what a Christian's life should be."

"Yeah, but all to no purpose."

"Wrong. Her faith and spiritual fortitude deepened by the hour. And after many years, long years, her prayers were finally answered. At last Ferdinand saw how low he had sunk, what a terrible life he had been leading. He repented of his sins, returned to the Church, and vowed a lead a more amiable life."

"And he did?"

"He did. His reform came a bit late, but the last years of Rita's married life were warm and comfortable and happy. Unfortunately, during the course of his bad years, Ferdinand had made as many enemies as friends. Though the news of his miraculous change spread rapidly, these enemies saw no reason to stop hating him. When he approached them, they accepted his embrace and his apologies while all the time planning their revenge. They had it at last. While away from home, Ferdinand was taken by surprise and brutally murdered.

"Rita's grief can hardly be described. After eighteen years of marriage, she suddenly found herself alone, with only the Church and her two teenage sons to console her."

"And the sons weren't much of a consolation."

"They were at first. They had loved their father, and they mourned his death as she did. But all too soon their thoughts turned to revenge."

"Uh-oh."

"They couldn't get to work right away. Their father had a lot of enemies, as I mentioned before, and they couldn't go out and kill all of them. But they slowly narrowed down the list until they were sure they had found their father's killer."

"How'd they figure out who dunnit?"

"Fair means and foul. They knew their father's friends and the sons of his friends. A few well-placed questions and a few gold coins worked wonders. As soon as they were certain, they began to plot the murderer's murder.

"Rita overheard her boys talking over their scheme, another shock to her nervous system at a time when she could scarecely bear it. She broke into their room—something she had never done before, as she was a great respecter of privacy—and demanded to know exactly what they planned to do.

"Her sons were reluctant to give her any details, but they confessed that the gist of what she had overheard was true: they had every intention of committing the mortal sin of murder to avenge their father's death.

"Rita begged them to reconsider. She pointed out that vengeance is not for humans to enact but best left in God's hands. Deliberate murder is a sin that condemns the sinner to hell. In fact, just by considering murder so seriously, they were balancing near the brink of eternal torment.

"Her sons rejected her reasoning. They had never accepted their mother's religious principles, and they weren't about to start now. After they had carried out their plan, there would be time enough to see about reforming their lives."

"You bet they'd have time; they'd be in jail for life."

"Not necessarily. Remember that Ferdinand's murderer was still at large. There was no metropolitan police force in Rocca Porena. More likely than not, they would never be caught."

"Maurice, you said 'would never.' Does that mean they didn't kill the guy?"

"No, they didn't."

"Mom talked them out of it, huh?"

Maurice was quiet for so long that I had to look up to make sure he was still there. His serious face scared me. A grim angel is nothing to giggle at.

"Maurice? Are you okay?"

"I'm not sure you're ready for what happens next. At the time it wasn't *too* awful; but now you'll probably think it's hideous."

"What happened?"

"Rita went to God with her troubles, as she always did. She begged Him to change the hearts and souls of her sons before they could commit this crime. And if they could not be moved . . . she asked God to take them to Himself before they could sin."

"You mean . . . kill them?"

"In a word, yes."

"Wow!"

Rita overheard her boys talking.

St. Rita

"Gian and Paolo fell ill with a fatal fever. Before they died, they repented of the sin they had almost committed and, thus, passed on in the peace of God."

"If they repented, Maurice, why did they have to die?"

"I can't answer that," Maurice said quietly. "God knows. Maybe He knew that though the boys might repent now, when the fear of death was upon them, they would regret their decision as soon as they returned to health and quickly carry out their original plan."

It was my turn to be quiet for a while.

"Rita loved her sons, didn't she?"

"Yes, she did."

"And yet she could pray for their deaths?"

"She prefered heaven to earth, and the afterlife to the life before. She didn't want her sons to go to hell. If they could not stay in the world and keep from sin, it was better that they should die before condemning themselves to eternal torment."

"It still seems a little extreme to me."

"Rita may have felt the same way. But she accepted God's will and thanked Him through her tears for having answered her prayers."

"But if she had never prayed for such a thing in the first place . . ."

"Probably the same thing would have happened. Or it may not have happened." Maurice's tone warned me that we were getting close to one of those topics we weren't supposed to talk about.

"So what happened after her sons died?"

"After the traditional mourning period had passed, Rita disposed of all her worldly goods and headed for the cloister at Cascia, where she asked to be admitted to the life of a nun. Several times she was refused because of her age—thirty-two—and because the convent was open only to virgins, not to previously married women. But at last her patience and persistence paid off. She was finally able to live the life she had always desired."

"I finished my notes and put my pencil down. My eyes kept returning to the passage where Rita had prayed for her sons. Her prayer for their deaths seemed cold, heartless. Yet she had loved them dearly. She had done it, to use an old-fashioned phrase, "to save their souls." And salvation is reckoned to be more important than life itself. Still . . .

"I felt Maurice's hand rest gently on my shoulder. "They are all happy in heaven now," he said. Then he added, "I'll see you tomorrow."

"Goodbye, Maurice."

He left quietly.

ST. FRANCIS OF SALES

"Good morning," said Maurice very gently.

"Morning," I managed.

"*Still* brooding about St. Rita?" Maurcie teased, but I could tell that he was also concerned.

"Yeah, I guess. Sorry."

"Nothing to be sorry for. Shall we move on to someone more cheerful?"

"Yeah. Can we do St. Francis of Sales?"

"Excellent choice. St. Francis of Sales is the patron of Catholic journalists and, thus, of Catholic writers, whose august body you aspire to join. He's also slightly different from the other saints we've seen. They were sure of their vocations at the tenderest of ages. But Francis didn't have half as much trouble with his parents as he did with himself."

"Oh?" I began to feel a stir of improved interest.

"Did you think you were the only one who has had trouble discovering God's plan for your life?"

Maurice's smile prompted one of my own.

"Listen and learn." Maurice tilted back so that his body formed a forty-five degree angle, a sure sign that a long story was ahead.

"Francis was born in 1513 in Sales, which his father, Francis, was count of, and which his mother, Frances of Sionas, was countess of. She was fifteen when her firstborn child came into the world. Her husband, a gruff old fellow who was both a soldier and a diplomat—whichever was necessary—was almost three times her age. Small wonder that she often got along better with her children than with her spouse.

"Francis grew up in the great, drafty chateau, or castle, of Sales, which was home to about forty people: relatives, servants, friends, guests, and others. But Francis didn't have to journey far to find privacy. The chateau was surrounded by a thick, quiet woods where one's peace was interrupted only by deer, rabbits, and, oh yes, an occasional bear or wolf.

"The count had grand plans for his little boy. Young Francis would start as a soldier, as his father had, and work his way up in the service of his government. The countess had other ideas. A quiet and pious woman, she worked hard to bring Francis to a knowledge of God. She took him along when she delivered food to the hungry or tried to comfort the ailing. She taught him the prayers of her childhood, and each night she would read to him from the Bible or some other holy book.

"As Francis grew, he dreamed of someday becoming a priest and doing the things his mother so admired, but he kept his dream a secret. He feared his father's disfavor more than he feared the wolves that sometimes howled under his window at night.

"Though Francis never mentioned what he hoped to become, he managed to convince his father of what he did *not* hope to become—a soldier. He was too serious, too quiet . . ."

"Too intelligent?"

"You said it, I didn't. Too quiet . . . to become a martial leader of men. As an alternative and almost equally glorious career, his father decided upon the law. As a lawyer, Francis would have the opportunity to become involved in politics and someday, perhaps, become a powerful voice in the government of Savoy."

"But as a future count, didn't he already have a voice in the government?"

"Not a very loud one. And not a very secure one, with the Calvinist upheavals surrounding them."

"Where is Savoy?"

"In what you now call Switzerland.

"The Calvinist upheavals are worth mentioning in a little more detail, as Francis would spend much of his life doing spiritual battle with them. They had succeeded in disrupting—even destroying—the Catholics from the country north of Sales as far as Lake Geneva and beyond. Everyone talked of the Protestant threat. Many an evening after supper, Francis would linger near the warmth of the fire and hear the grown-ups speak of the razing of churches, the killings of priests, the flight of desperate refugees. Such conversations made a deep impression on young Francis.

"One time, when he was still a boy—I don't think he was more than five years old—he heard that his father was playing host to a Calvinist visitor."

"Knowingly?"

"Possibly. He may have been a brother or cousin or someone the count didn't want to offend. But Francis was offended, and excited too. To think that the terrible enemy was actually within his home!

"He ran outside to the hen house, used a big stick to band the flock together, and herded them right to the front gate while yelling his battle cry: 'Come on! Come on! At 'em, the heretics!' —What's so funny?"

"I'm sorry," I wheezed, holding my aching sides. "It's just that I see a little boy with tousled blond hair, waving a stick taller than his head, and leading an army of chi-chi-*chickens*!"

"And you think that's funny?"

I couldn't stop laughing long enough to give Maurice an answer. Maurice almost grinned. I *saw* him.

"Did it—did it work?" I asked, when I could talk.

"No, it didn't."

"The army laid an egg, eh?"

Maurice folded his arms over his chest and refused to look at me until I sat up straight again.

"Are you quite through?"

"Quite." I coughed.

"May we proceed?"

"Yes, I think so."

"I hope you realize that the Calvinist crusade was no laughing matter."

32

St. Francis of Sales

"Yes, I do."

"And I trust that your undignified outburst will not repeat itself."

"Not unless you mention you-know-whats again."

"I won't."

"When Francis was seven years old, he was sent off to boarding school at La Roche, despite his mother's protests. She was sure that her little boy would never survive the separation from home, not to mention the rough company of boys who weren't quite as well brought up as he was."

"Do I detect a note of the overprotective mother?"

"One *could* say that," Maurice allowed. "Also, Francis had had his share of childhood illnesses, which caused the countess great anxiety. What she forgot to consider was that her son was familiar with the country skills of hunting, fishing, and riding, and that he was well equipped to defend himself should the need arise."

"So Francis didn't have any problems at school?"

"I didn't say that. He had fights with fists and feelings, but he got through them as well as other boys did. He was that rare combination, a serious student and a popular classmate."

"Ah, yes. I know how hard it is to be both at the same time."

Maurice did smile then.

"Francis," he continued, "would have been perfectly happy to stay at La Roche. But when La Roche seemed likely to be the site of a major battle between the Calvinists and the duke of Savoy, he was quickly transferred to a school at Annecy, which was safer and closer to home.

"Life was quiet and studious and fairly uneventful for Francis until he graduated from Annecy at the age of fifteen. He knew where he wanted to continue his studies: the University College of Clermont in Paris, famed for its stern Jesuit teachers and its demanding course of study. After careful consideration, the count agreed to send him there.

"So, in 1528, Francis mounted his horse and made the long journey to Paris, accompanied by his private tutor, Abbé Déage."

"Ah-hah! A private tutor! No wonder he did so well in school."

"The tutor helped," Maurice admitted, "but I submit that Francis would have been a brilliant student if he'd been shut up in a library with no teacher at all. His tutor demanded more of him than his most difficult professors. To satisfy him, Francis had to stretch his brain to the utmost. Brain stretching, I might add, is an exercise that should be more popular than it is."

"Don't look at me in that tone of voice, Maurice. *I* watch public television."

"While Francis busied himself with his studies, his tutor worked on his own doctorate in theology, trusting his pupil to do his work alone. His grades didn't falter without Déage's help. He balanced work time and playtime equally well."

"*Playtime!* Saints *play*?"

"Of course they play. At least Francis did. He attended dances, drank the health of fair ladies, and enjoyed the company of his peers, both in and out of the classroom. He didn't always approve of some of their hangouts—Paris had a few unsavory cabarets at the time—but he didn't adopt a holier-than-thou attitude, even though he was. He earned the good favor of God and man without offending either."

"A feat comparable to walking a tightrope without a net."

"Francis's mind expanded, and his love and understanding of God grew without hindrance until he was nineteen. Then he fell into what may be called a dark night of the soul.

"Up to this year, 1586, he had devoted himself to earthly subjects—history, languages, philosophy, art, and so on. Now, with the end of his university years in sight, he decided to move on to theology. He was particularly interested in Catholic answers to Calvinist questions. Almost immediately he discovered the topic of predestination. Do you know what predestination is, girl in the front row?"

I stood up. "Predestination is the doctrine which holds that God has already decided who shall go to heaven and who shall go to hell, and that nothing a person does will change his fate."

"Good enough. Sit down.

"Francis seized hold of this slippery doctrine and wrestled with it. Man has free will. He can accept God's will and guidance, or he can reject them. But God knows everything. God knows who will be His people and who will turn from Him. So if God knows what you will do before you do it, do you really have free will? If God knows you're going to hell, what's the use of struggling to save yourself? In a sinful world, is anyone worthy to be saved? Is anyone free from the taint of sin? Does anyone deserve salvation?"

"Maurice, you want to know something? You're making me dizzy."

"But I'm still at the beginning, young one. Francis went a lot deeper than that. And the deeper he got, the more lost he became. He turned to the writings of St. Augustine and St. Thomas Aquinas for help, but he didn't find what he needed. It even seemed to him that these Doctors of the Church were in agreement with the Calvinists! They said that God dispenses His grace to those He wishes to save. If God does not intend to number you among the elect, neither faith nor good works can keep you from hell.

"For the entire winter of 1586-1587, Francis lived in an agony of confusion. He wondered if he was counted among the damned, if all the prayers and sacrifices he offered to God had no meaning at all. His spiritual sickness took its toll on his body. Déage worried about him. But Francis told no one, not even his tutor, of his terror.

"The only rock Francis could cling to was his firm conviction of God's love. In spite of his dread of damnation, he couldn't turn away from his heavenly Father. Nor was he presumptuous enough to consider himself to be among the elect. At one point he wrote: 'Whatever happens, Lord, may I at least love You in this life if I cannot love You in eternity, since no one may praise You in hell. May I at least make use of every moment of my short life on earth to love You.'"

"You're saying that Francis never stopped loving God, even when he believed that God had condemned him?"

"Never. He *did* suffer a loss of hope, of trust. But he never doubted God's justice and love.

"Finally, one day after classes, Francis resolved to settle his problem for once and for all. He went to the church of St. Etienne-des-Grès, knelt in the Lady Chapel, and prayed in his own words:

> Whatever happens, O Lord, You hold everything in Your hands, and all Your ways are just and true. Though You have veiled my eyes before the eternal secret of predestination and reprobation, You whose judgments are unsearchable, You who are ever a just Judge and a merciful Father, I shall love You, Lord, at least in this life, even if I am not allowed to love you in eternity.... And if it is inevitable that I must be among the damned who will never see Your gentle face, let me at least be spared from the company of those who will curse Your holy name.

When he had finished this prayer, his eyes fell upon a holy card that someone had left in the chapel. Automatically, he read the words: *Remember, O most gracious Virgin Mary, that never was it known...*

"As he read on, an incredible feeling of peace and protection came over him. His doubts and fears for the future fled like uncaged birds. His trial had ended. God had restored him to health."

"Mentally as well as spiritually?"

"You mean, did he find the answers to his questions?"

"Uh, yeah."

"He found one answer that satisfied him. In concentrating on God's justice, he had totally forgotten to consider God's mercy. When that concept was added into his reasoning, he felt much better. He was sure now that God did not condemn anyone to eternal torment. People go to hell of their own accord."

"I guess that settled that."

"For the moment. The question of predestination would come up again in Francis's life, but it would never torment him as it had during his college days in Paris.

"Francis graduated—gloriously, I may add—in 1588. The very next day he was off for home, his faithful tutor riding by his side. When they reached his family's new residence, a chateau near Geneva, Francis found that he had a great deal of catching up to do. Not only had the four siblings he knew—Gallois, Louis, Jean-Francois, and Gasparde—grown a great deal in the past six years, he now had three little brothers he had never seen: Bernard, Melchior, and Janus.

"The graduate was given a hero's welcome. While he enthralled the folks at home with tales of life in exotic Paris, they gave him the news of what had happened at home in the wild country he loved."

"Is this where Francis tells his father about his plan to become a priest?"

"Not yet. Even though he was twenty-one years old and currently held in high esteem by his parents, he hesitated to speak of his vocation. Maybe he wasn't sure of it yet. Maybe he still feared his father's wrath; the old man had not mellowed with age. In any case, when the count suggested that Francis should continue his studies and become a doctor of law, Francis obeyed. Later that same year, he left for Padua, Italy, accompanied by Déage and by Francis's oldest brother, Gallois, who was to study at the Jesuit school in the same city.

"The years at Padua weren't as tumultuous as the years at Paris. Francis met a man who was to be a major spiritual influence, the Jesuit priest Antonio Possevino. When he told his new friend about his struggle with the problem of predestination, Possevino advised him not to dwell on the subject until he could study it in more detail, that is, until he had his degree. Francis took his advice.

"The pain he suffered in Padua was physical rather than spiritual, and almost as deadly. Caught in the typhoid epidemic of the summer of 1590, Francis was still seriously ill in January. After Possevino administered extreme unction, now known as the sacrament of the sick, Francis regained his health.

"In 1591, Francis graduated with the usual honors and praises. One of his teachers predicted that he would be 'the luminary of his century.'

"After making a grand tour of Italy, including visits to Loretto and Rome, he rejoined his family. The battles in the Chablais between

St. Francis of Sales

Calvinists and Catholics had obliged them to move to La Thuile, south of Lake Annecy."

"It sounds as if Francis's family moved every time he left home."

"But they always wrote to tell him where they were."

"Wonder if my family would," I mused. But Maurice ignored that comment and went on with the story.

"His father was as pleased as the proverbial punch that his oldest boy had already established such a brilliant reputation. He presented him with a complete legal library as a graduation gift. Francis was deeply grateful. His gratitude made it all the more difficult to tell his father that he didn't plan to be a lawyer, that making a splendid marriage and stepping up to the bar of the Savoy senate were not among his goals."

"He's . . . twenty-four, right?"

"Twenty-five."

"And still keeping it a secret that he wants to be a priest!"

"Still not keen on upsetting his father."

"Seems to have a Jonah streak in him."

"And, like Jonah, he needed a miracle to push him into action."

"A whale swallowed him?"

"Not quite *that* dramatic a miracle. Dramatic enough though. Déage and Francis had gone to Chambery, the capital of Savoy, to see about Francis's appointment to the bar. On the way home, Francis fell off his horse. Not once, not twice, but three times. And each time he fell, his sword fell from its scabbard, and sword and scabbard landed on the ground in such a way that sword and scabbard formed a cross.

"This thrice-repeated sign convinced Francis that God wanted him to speak out at last. He promptly told the unsuspecting Déage about his dream of becoming a priest. The tutor was amazed. In all the years they had been together, he had never heard Francis even mention a vocation. But as he listened to the young man's fervent words, Déage could not doubt that Francis was being called to serve God as a priest. The question now was what to do next."

"Don't tell me that Déage, too, was afraid of the count."

"*Everyone* was afraid of the count. But the time to act had come. If the count was going to throw tantrums, curse his son, cast him out of the family, then so be it. Regardless of the consequences, the blow would have to be dealt. But maybe a way could be found to soften it.

"When they reached home, Francis visited his priest-cousin Canon Louis de Sales and asked for his assistance. He gave it, but not in the way Francis expected. Instead of breaking the news to the crusty count, Louis got in touch with the local bishop. With the bishop's permission,

Canon Louis placed his retiring cousin's name in nomination to the Pope for the provostship of the diocese."

"In other words, Louis went over the old man rather than through him."

"Precisely. And it worked. In May of 1593, the papal bull approving the bishop's choice arrived. Louis carried it off to La Thuile at once.

"It was hard to tell who was more amazed by this news, Francis or his father. But amazement soon gave way to the stormy scene Francis had dreaded for so long. Through the yelling and stamping, Louis rallied to his cousin's defense. He pointed out that the office of the provost was second only to that of the bishop and certainly a position of honor well suited to the son of a count. And the work would keep him close to the family and country he loved.

"Considering the terror he inspired in just about everyone, the count consented surprisingly soon. He wasn't happy about it, and he let Francis know exactly how disappointed he was: but if Francis was sure he wanted to be a priest, then a priest he could certainly be. He was old enough to make up his own mind.

"Francis was stunned by his father's consent. This wasn't exactly the mighty blowup he had feared all these years. Obviously he had misjudged the old man. In concentrating on his terrible temper, he had totally forgotten his awesome love."

"Sounds as if he made the same mistake with his earthly father as he did with his heavenly one."

"Shortly thereafter, Francis was ordained a priest and began his splendid and inspiring career."

"At the age of twenty-six."

"Better late than never. I could go on forever...."

"It feels as if you already have, Maurice."

"But Francis's life story could fill up several books, and we *do* have some more saints to talk about."

"Not today we don't, Maurice. We'll carry on tomorrow."

"As you wish."

"Maurice, wait!"

"Yes?"

"Before you go, could you help me get this pencil from between my fingers? I seem to have contracted a severe case of writer's cramp."

"Easily cured by an angel's touch," Maurice said loftily.

And it was.

ST. JOHN CALYBITES

Guardian angels are supposed to be on call twenty-four hours a day, *every* day; but try getting one between two and three in the morning.

I had to pray persistently for almost five minutes before Maurice even started to fade in.

"What is it?" he demanded peevishly.

"Did I wake you up?"

"Angels never have to sleep."

"But were you?"

He might have been tempted to deny it if a big yawn hadn't taken him by surprise.

"Fine thing, Mr. Guardian Angel. I can't even close my eyes, but you're Up There, snoring blissfully away."

"Angels don't snore," Maurice claimed, and as I've never seen—or heard—a snoring angel, I couldn't argue with him.

"Since I can't get to sleep, Maurice, we might as well get some work done. Can you think of a saint with a short story and a happy ending?"

"I can think of a saint with a short story and a *fairly* happy ending."

"Okay, G.A., let's hear it."

"Aren't you going to write it down?"

"I'll write it down in the morning."

"You'll forget it by morning. Write it down now."

"I don't feel like getting out of bed."

Maurice popped pencil and paper into my lap. For a guardian angel, he's pretty human at times.

"Thanks, Guardian."

"Don't expect me to do that *all* the time," Maurice groused. "I wouldn't have done it this time if you didn't look so pathetic. Those rings under your eyes make you look like a half-masked racoon."

"Thanks again."

"Now just lean back, relax, and listen while Uncle Maurice tells you a bedtime story."

"John was born in Constantinople in the early half of the fifth century. In spite of the family wealth, he discovered God at an early age."

"Doesn't everyone?"

"His parents didn't object to his religious interest. As a matter of fact, at his request, they gave him a book of the Gospels for a present. It was a beautiful book, bound in gold. But more precious to John were the golden words inside it.

"John didn't think about the question of his vocation for some years. Then one day, an abbot came to his house to visit John's father and take a break from his pilgrimage to Jerusalem. John listened to his stories of monastery life: the hardships and the holiness, the solitude and silent fellowship. He was entranced. He had a chance to talk to the abbot in private before he left. John got the abbot to stop by on his return journey and take him to join the pious men he spoke of."

"He must have been a pretty fast talker."

"I think it was more his sincerity and dedication that impressed the abbot. But whatever it was, the abbot kept his word. He returned in several weeks' time. John was ready. He had packed some clothes and the golden Gospel book in a little pack. In secret, he slipped away from the house, fearing his father's wrath and his mother's sorrow."

"You mean he didn't even leave a note?"

"Not a word. He didn't want to be followed and brought back."

"Didn't the kid know how upset they would be?"

"Yes, he knew. But he had read that to follow Jesus, one must leave one's father and mother, take up one's cross, and not look back."

"I don't think Jesus would have been too upset if he'd left a *little* note."

"Go back and read St. Luke, chapter 14, and you might think differently. Now, where were we? Oh, yes. After a long and difficult journey, the abbot and the boy reached their destination: Gomon on the Bosphorous, the home of 'the Sleepless Monks'—"

"I could join that outfit myself, tonight."

"—which was founded by St. Alexander Akimetes. The monastery was as tough and trying as it sounds, an excellent place for strengthening one's spiritual fiber."

"Assuming that one's physical fiber is up to it."

"John lived happily there for six years, devoting himself to the service of God and to the monks who lived with him. But after his sixth year, a curious thing happened. John suddenly became seriously homesick. He longed to be with his parents again, to see the city he had loved. He begged his superior for guidance. Should he leave the monastery and risk not being able to return? Or should he remain and risk dying of his longing?"

"*That* serious, Maurice?"

"That serious."

"Mm."

"You were about to say something?"

"Just that I can't imagine anyone dying of homesickness. But I'll take your word for it."

Pray that you'll never have to find out for yourself someday. After much prayer, the superior advised him to go home, trusting God to bring his young friend's adventures to a happy end."

"How old is John, by the way?"

Maurice scratched his left eyebrow. "I'm not at all sure. I don't think he was much over twenty when he died. Might even have been below it.

"John set out joyfully for home, his pack slung lightly over his back. When he was half way there, he met up with a beggar, who looked enviously at the young man's snug apparel. John offered to change clothes with him. He didn't have to suggest it twice."

"You know what I'm thinking, Maurice? I figure that there was more to that swap than simple Christian charity."

"You may have a point there, young one. During the long walk, John had begun to wonder if his parents would truly be gald to see him. He had left them rather abruptly, after all. He decided to approach them as a stranger first, to see what sort of a welcome he would receive."

"But the welcome people give to a stranger is a lot different from the welcome they give to a son."

"Shouldn't be," said Maurice, rather innocently.

" 'Tis," said I.

"In his beggar's rags, his face smirched with dirt," Maurice continued, "John came home. With rapidly beating heart, he knocked at the old familiar door. His mother opened it. She stared at him. Her nose wrinkled in disgust. Then she slammed the door in his dirty face.

"John stood there for a moment or two. Then he turned and left his home again."

I'll bet he dumped his rags in a hurry and came back as himself."

"No."

"Oh. Well, then he returned to the monastery."

"No."

"What, then?"

"He moved into a nearby hovel, a *kalybe* in Greek. He stayed there for three years, devoting himself to prayer and good works. His parents would give him food. Even though she didn't know who he was, his mother repented of the way she had slammed the door in his dirty face, especially as news of his goodness reached her. But neither of his parents ever recognized him as their son. They thought he was a nice lad who had fallen on hard times.

"For three years John lived in solitude, though not the sort of solitude he knew at Gomon. At last, when he felt death close upon him, he decided to reveal his identity to his family. He sent for his mother, and when she came, he showed her the gold-bound Gospels he had been given so long ago. Only then did she know her son.

"His parents joyfully welcomed him home. They spent three wonderful days together. Then John died."

"That's your idea of a happy ending?" I yawned.

"I said '*fairly* happy,'" Maurice reminded me. "After all, he died at home with his parents."

"But he could have lived with them for three years instead of keeping his identity a secret and living in a hovel."

"He had God's work to do, and he didn't feel he could do it at home."

"Mm." I yawned again. "You've worn me out, Maurice. Thanks. G'night."

I suppose he left right after I fell asleep. I trust he did. In spite of his many faults, Maurice *is* a gentleman. Besides, what reason would he have to linger near a half-masked racoon? ◈

ST. JOAN OF VALOIS

"May *I* suggest a saint today?"

"Be my guest, Maurice," I said graciously. Now that we were half way through the book, I could afford to be gracious.

"Thank you. I'd like you to write about St. Joan."

"St. Joan of Arc?" I grabbed the nearest pencil. "Fantastic! I've been a fan of hers for years."

"St. Joan of Valois, also known as Jeanne de Valois, or Joan of France."

I put the pencil down. "Who?"

Maurice nodded glumly. "That's what everyone says. That's why I want you to write about her. Her story deserves to be told."

"Did she help Joan of Arc save France?"

"No."

"Did she work miracles?"

"No."

"Did she write books?"

"No."

"What *did* she do?"

"Eventually, she founded an order of nuns."

"Oh."

"But it's her life prior to that act that I want you to write about: the life of a French princess."

"Oh!"

"But not the kind of life you're thinking of."

"Oh."

"Shall I begin?"

" 'Go on . . . I'll follow thee.' "

"When the son of Charles VII took the French throne as Louis XI, he already had one child, Anne of France. What he most desired was a son to whom he could pass on the crown."

"Male chauvinist..."

" 'Twas the custom of the time, milady. He advised his wife of his desire, and Charlotte of Savoy, in three year's time, became pregnant."

"Kept him in suspense, huh?"

"And nearly endangered her own life, as she discovered when she gave birth to another daughter."

"Joan?"

"Joan."

"Don't tell me; let me guess. Lovely though she was, Joan was *only a girl*, so of course she wasn't good enough for Louis."

"Much of that is true. But lovely she wasn't. She was small, and not attractive. In fact, she was deformed."

"In what way?"

"I'd rather not be specific, if you don't mind. She suffered enough while she was on earth. Let your readers draw their own pictures."

"Some of them might be pretty grotesque."

"The readers or the pictures?"

"The pictures," I growled.

"So be it," said Maurice with a superior air. "I refuse to give in to the public fascination with freaks and misfits. Let them look to themselves."

"As soon as you jump off the soapbox, Friend Angel, we can get on with the story."

"Very well then. When Joan was eight days old, she was betrothed, as was also the custom, to Louis, the son of the duke of Orleans and Mary of Cleaves. This took place on the nineteenth of May in 1464. On that day, the baby was dispatched to live with her future parents-in-law."

"Also the custom?"

"No. But the king was furious at his wife's 'failure.' He ordered the baby away from court, and the queen was too terrified to disobey.

"Joan did not see her mother and father again until she was four years old. At Louis's command, her guardians then took her to Plessis-le-Tours.

"Her mother, seeing a lonely and gentle child, loved her at once and welcomed her into her arms. Her father saw only her ugliness. He made no secret of how offensive he found her. After a brief visit with her mother, Joan was sent back to her foster home.

"But her banishment wasn't sufficient for Louis. When he learned that his younger daughter often visited churches and chapels and found great comfort in the presence of God, he ordered the duke of Orleans to keep her out of all such places."

"Why?"

"Because he didn't like her. And also, I suspect, because he wasn't particularly religious himself, and didn't like being out-holied by a four-year-old."

"Sounds like a *baby* could have out-holied *him*!"

"Even *you* could have out-holied him."

"Thanks a bunch."

"Joan was banned from church, but no man on earth could ban her from prayer and private study. She satisfied herself with what she had, and tried to still the longing in her heart.

"When she was six years old, indirect relief came to her in the birth of her brother. Louis had his son at last. He was so pleased that, not only did he allow Joan to visit churches again, he even invited her to live with him at court."

"Where she should have been all along."

"Louis's court was a splendid place—you must have seen pictures of it in your history books. But Joan was not happy there. True, she could go to Mass every day if she wanted to, and she was not without friends in addition to her mother, sister, and brother. But her father still despised her. Every time he looked at her, his hatred grew. He knew that a number of people of the court—the countess of Linières in particular—treated her cruelly and with open contempt, but he did nothing about it."

"I'm surprised he didn't have her killed."

"He *did* try to kill her, once. I don't remember now what inspired him, if I can use such a word, but he once stormed her room with a sword in his hand and announced that he would kill her. Luckily for Joan, the count of Linières was nearby. Unlike his wife, the count had become fond of the crippled girl and treated her with true Christian compassion, a virtue in short supply in France at that time. He threw himself between Joan and her rampaging father and saved her life."

"Was he killed?"

"No. But in spite of his valiant effort, Joan was wounded. Soon she recovered, but the scar remained with her forever."

"Physical or mental?"

"Both. Good came of the incident though. Louis was ashamed of his rash act, as well he should have been, and gave Joan more freedom than she had ever known before. On some days she even got to go outside,

The count threw himself between Joan and her rampaging father.

St. Joan of Valois

though not where anyone could see her. It wouldn't do for the populace to discover that the king had fathered an imperfect child."

"So he was kinder to her after he tried to murder her?"

"Not as kind as he could have been. He still hated her beyond all reason and saw to it that their paths never crossed.

"When Joan had passed her twelfth birthday, she was married to her fiancé, the duke of Orleans. He was two years older than she. Joan did not marry him willingly, but she knew that worse things would happen to her if she resisted the king. She had no choice but to make the best of the situation. At worst, her husband could treat her no more cruelly than her father had."

"Which shows how little Joan knew about married life."

"You're jumping to conclusions."

"Uh-oh! I have a hunch that Joan did not live happily ever after."

"Joan did not see her husband very often. When he was at home, he took his cue from his king and treated her contemptibly—if he treated her at all. He spent most of his time in the court, in company with the beautiful and accomplished people whom he considered his equals. Sometimes a friend would ask him why he didn't bring his wife along. Wasn't he worried about leaving her alone in her rooms with so many raffish rogues hanging about? His answer was that he wasn't worried at all; his wife's shortness and plain face would defend her from all dangers."

'What charming wit. The marriage didn't last long, I hope?"

"Twenty-two years."

"Gads! I've already lived a year longer in semi-happiness than she lived in constant misery."

"And not uneventful misery either. Louis XI, Joan's sweet father, died in August of 1483. His son succeeded him to the throne, taking the title of Charles VIII. As he was a bit young to take official charge of the government, his older sister, Anne, served as regent until 1491, when he took power into his own hands.

"This arrangement did not please everyone. Most notably, it did not please the duke of Orleans. Since Anne was otherwise occupied, married to Peter of Bourbon, the duke felt that the crown should have gone to him, as he was married to the second-oldest child. He tried to stir up trouble. In fact, he stirred up quite a bit of trouble, which necessitated his flight to Brittany. There he joined forces with Duke Francis II, Charles's favorite enemy. War broke out shortly thereafter."

"What a mess, Maurice! With her brother on one side and her husband on the other, poor Joan was really caught in the middle."

"And she used her position to try to bring the two sides to a peaceful settlement. Twice she used her influence to get her husband out of French jails. The first time, he hightailed it back to Brittany. The second time, he behaved himself and stayed home.

"When Charles died on the seventh of April in 1498, Joan's husband realized his dream. He was crowned Louis XII. Scarcely was he settled on the throne before he began to petition the Pope to annul his marriage."

"*That's* gratitude for you! After all Joan did for him—"

" '—the least he could do would be to let her reign as his queen.' Is that your point?"

"Exactly, Maurice. The very least."

"Or, to look at it another way, the least he could do would be to give her her freedom after twenty-two years of bother and neglect."

"Well . . . for *me*, a few years of queendom could make up for an awful lot of neglect."

"You wouldn't think so if you had been there. But, to get on with the business at hand, Louis XII claimed that his marriage should be annulled because he had been forced into it, which was true, and because the union had never been consummated, which was also true. Pope Alexander VI decided in his favor."

"Very interesting, Maurice. How did Joan take the divorce?"

"The opinion you get on that depends on whom you read. Some writers claim that Joan fought the proceedings every step of the way. Others say that she let Louis do what he wanted. She had waited a long time for her freedom. This seemed the best way—perhaps the only way—to get it."

"Okay, Guardian Angel, what's the inside story?"

"I offer to you as evidence that Joan took the final decision so well that Louis felt a little ashamed of himself. To express his gratitude and soothe his conscience, he made his ex-wife the duchess of Berry and also gave her charge of Pontoise and a few other townships."

"Joan didn't remain at court then."

"Would you?"

"Unh-uh. No. Not if I'd been treated that way."

"She retired to Bourges, where she devoted her generous heart and substantial revenues to works of charity."

"What happened to Louis?"

"As soon as the divorce was final, he married Anne of Brittany, the widow of Joan's brother."

"Didn't lose much time, did he?"

"History doesn't judge Louis XII as harshly as you seem to. He was one of the most popular French kings. Known as the Father of the People, he introduced long-needed financial and judicial reforms, and was noted for the mildness of his rule."

"At least he wasn't as . . . unpleasant as Louis XI."

"Let me put it this way, young one. Most *Huns* weren't as unpleasant as Louis XI."

"I take it that Joan spent the rest of her days in peace."

"In peace, prayer, and good works. In 1500, one of her fondest dreams came true when she founded the Annonciades, an Order of nuns especially devoted to Our Lady. She took the habit herself on Pentecost in 1504 and died on the fourth day of February in 1505."

"At the age of, umm, forty."

"Your math is getting better."

"She packed an awful lot of life into less than half a century."

"An awful lot of pain too," Maurice reminded me.

"Yeah. Thanks for suggesting her. You get good ideas sometimes."

"Maybe that'll teach you to listen to me more often."

ST. CLARE

"You're pouting already," Maurice observed. "That's a bad sign."

"We've done a run of unfamiliar saints. Can we go back to the familiar ones now?"

"Like who?"

"Like St. Francis. Of *Assisi*," I added quickly. I don't get caught the same way thrice."

"*Everyone* knows about St. Francis," said Maurice reasonably. "Why don't you take St. Clare instead?"

"St. Clare had problems?"

"St. Clare had problems. You'll like her. She wasn't as submissive as the other young women have been."

"You mean she didn't get married?"

"She didn't."

"Tell me all about her."

"Clare was born in 1193 to Phavorino Sciffo, a noble knight, and his wife, Hortulaha, an equally noble woman. They quickly became the No. 1 family in Assisi, in central Italy. The Sciffos were noted for their religious devotion as well as for their wealth and physical attractiveness."

"Maurice, I'm getting tired of all these rich people."

"Don't blame me. It's not my fault that poor kids don't have as much trouble as rich kids."

"Come again?"

"Poor parents are more likely to let their kids become their own people. Rich parents want their kids to have all the advantages money can buy—whether they want them or not."

"Mm. I'd argue with you, Maurice, but I don't have any personal experience to fall back on. However, if you could arrange for my parents to find the pot of gold at the end of the rainbow . . ."

St. Clare

"Sorry. That's not my job.

"As I'm sure you've already guessed, Clare inherited her parents' religious fervor. She was generous with her allowance, faithful in prayer, and an excellent example to her two younger sisters, Agnes and Beatrice. One couldn't ask for a more devoted daughter. One *might* wish, however, that she were a little less . . . headstrong, a little less inclined to immerse herself totally in new ideas. Her parents thought this a dangerous tendency and resolved, instead, to channel her energies into respectable marriage as soon as possible."

"So, at the tender age of twelve . . ."

"No, no. This is a different world from the ones we've seen before. Assisi wasn't Rocca Porena or Rome. Clare was eighteen before her parents began seriously to husband hunt."

"Eighteen! She's practically an old maid!"

"Coming from someone who's unmarried at twenty-three . . ."

"Don't rush me, pal."

"Clare knew what her mother and father were up to. But she had no intention of being forced into marriage. She would be Christ's bride alone. But she needed help. She needed to know God's will. She needed sincere spiritual advice. Where could she find it?"

"The suspense is killing me."

"She had heard of a remarkable man—all of Assisi had heard of a remarkable man—named Francis. Like her, he had been born into a wealthy family. As she planned to do, he had left his father's house to embrace a life of poverty and prayer. He sounded like the perfect counselor. So, in the company of an older female friend, of course, she journeyed out of the city to meet him. It wouldn't do for a young lady to visit a young man alone."

"Heavens, no. Proprieties must be observed."

"Francis welcomed her with the warmth he extended to all God's creatures. His gentle face, his kind eyes, the depth and truth of his holy love brought peace to Clare's troubled soul. They discovered that they shared much in common, that they agreed on many things, chief among them that Clare must leave home before her parents announced her betrothal. They set the date and made their plans. Then Clare and her friend, who could be trusted to keep her mouth shut, returned to Assisi.

"The eighteenth of March seemed a Palm Sunday like any other. Clare dressed in her finest clothes and went with her family to church in the morning. The rest of the day passed in rejoicing and feasting in anticipation of the holy day ahead. Clare was especially sweet and kind to everyone.

"That night, after her parents and sisters had fallen asleep, Clare left the house, met her cousin Pacifica (the friend mentioned earlier), and hurried to the little chapel in the woods at Portiuncula, where Francis and his followers were living.

"The two girls were warmly welcomed and brought to the chapel altar. Here Francis cut their hair—as a sign of their union with Christ—and gave them coarse Franciscan tunics to wear over their clothes. After prayer and holy festivity, everyone went to bed."

"Ahem."

"The women slept in the chapel, and the men retired to another part of the forest."

"Thank you."

"Clare and Pacifica would have been blissfully happy to live with the brothers and share their difficult life, begging from door to door and preaching the word of God. But Francis knew that would never do. People would jump to the same conclusion you so crudely jumped to a few moments ago. (It's alarming how little human nature has changed over the centuries.) So, after morning Mass, Francis took the two girls to St. Paul's, a Benedictine convent near Bastia.

"Meanwhile, back at Assisi, Clare's parents were upset over her disappearance. Her father guessed where she had gone. The next day, supported by various friends and relations, he stormed the chapel and demanded his daughter. The friars stood by as they searched the forest from top to bottom. They didn't deny that the girls had been there, but they wouldn't say where they were.

"Phavorino was no fool. He figured out fast that there was only one convent close enough for the girls to have reached in two days' time. The posse galloped off to Bastia and got to St. Paul's in record time.

"Clare and Pacifica heard them coming. They sought sanctuary in the convent chapel, behind the altar. The men might violate the sanctity of the convent, but they surely wouldn't trespass upon the table of the Lord.

"Clare had underestimated her father's anger. He led the march through the convent as easily as though it were a conquered village. The nuns held their ground as best they could, but it was only a matter of time until Phavorino and his men captured the chapel.

"Pacifica was willing to give up peacefully. But Clare wasn't about to go. When her father seized her to carry her away, she grabbed the altar cloths and dragged them with her. She shook off the hood of her habit to reveal her shorn head and told her father straight out that she would be no mortal man's bride. She belonged to Christ, and with Christ she would remain. If he wanted to take her home, he would have to carry her all the way. And when God gave her the opportunity, she would run away again.

"Her father informed her that she had disgraced the family and herself by her rash action. Running away from home was bad enough, but spending the night with that gang of supposedly holy hooligans was even worse. If she didn't repent of her folly and come home at once, her chance for a good marriage and the respect of people in the community would be gone for good.

"Clare informed her father that marriage and respectability were of no interest to her. She had chosen to follow Jesus through Francis, and she was of an age to make her own decisions. Now if he and his friends would kindly leave, she would go about her business. She *did* have things to do.

"Phavorino knew when he was licked. He left Clare and Pacifica where they were, hoping that a few days of convent life, with its austerity and hard routine, would cure Clare of her latest passion."

"Well, Maurice, there's one more example of a parent underestimating his child."

"Not child but children, as we shall soon see. The good sisters of St. Paul's had been rather distressed by this ugly scene. They began to wonder if it was such a good idea to have Clare and Pacifica on the premises.

Clare's family, remember, was rich and powerful. They could make a lot of trouble for one little convent.

"Clare and Pacifica were aware of the tension they were causing. In less than two weeks, they moved to the convent of Sant'Angelo-in-Panzo, which was located on the lovely slopes of Mount Subasio. Clare hoped that her father's influence wouldn't reach that far.

"For the first few weeks, it seemed she was right. No one came looking for her, and she looked for no one but God and, occasionally, Francis. But then, one otherwise peaceful day, her little sister Agnes suddenly appeared on the convent doorstep with her long hair cut short and a rough robe clutched tightly around her body. She announced that she had come to join them in their walk with Jesus.

"Clare and Pacifica welcomed her joyfully. The other nuns weren't quite so pleased. Agnes was only fourteen. Did her parents know where she was and what she had done?

"No, Agnes admitted, they did not."

"I'll bet they soon found out."

"If you think of the disturbance at St. Paul's as a battle, you should consider the encounter at Sant'Angelo-in-Panzo a full-scale war. Phavorino couldn't fight Clare, but no one would be allowed to dispute his right to little Agnes. These nuns were obviously keeping her prisoner. He would rescue her!

"His little army attacked the convent in the early hours of the morning, while most of the nuns were still asleep. In the midst of the screams, bellowings, and panic, Agnes was captured and taken away under loud protest. After a bit, she managed to escape and ran back to the convent, obliging her father to give up again."

"The old boy isn't very persistent, is he, Maurice?"

"You forget that Clare's family is pious as well as willful. After making the good old college try and finding himself rebuffed, Phavorino was willing to let his daughters be and hope God would bring them to their senses."

"Or him to his."

"The sisters at Sant'Angelo-in-Panzo cared even less for this invasion of privacy than the sisters at St. Paul's had. In hopes of silently persuading the three girls to seek a spiritual haven elsewhere, the nuns began to make life rather unpleasant for them.

"Francis realized that he would have to set up a real convent for them, a place where they could live by the Franciscan Rule without bothering anyone else. But no one in the Order had any money. They weren't *allowed* to have money."

St. Clare

"Well, Maurice, that's what happens when you take a vow of poverty."

"That vow solves as many problems as it causes. Francis turned to the Benedictines for help, as he had turned before. He wasn't disappointed. They gave him St. Damian's, a little church on the outskirts of Assisi, one of the churches Francis had repaired in the early days of his ministry. Clare, Pacifica, and Agnes moved in at once. Several of their friends soon followed them. They accepted Clare as the superior of their order. Clare, in turn, put herself and her friends under Francis's spiritual direction.

"Thus began the Second Order of St. Francis. And, with few changes, thus it remains to the present day."

"In the same little church?"

"Of course not. The Poor Clares, like the Franciscans, are known all over the world. St. Clare herself founded convents in Perugia, Arezzo, Padua, Rome, Venice, Mantua . . ."

"*I* know all that! I just wanted to make sure the readers did."

"They do now," Maurice said wisely, "and *you* do, too, in case you didn't before."

"I'd never lie. To an angel."

"Mmm," Maurice said, but he vanished before I could ask him what *Mmm* meant.

ST. MARTIN OF TOURS

I was rereading the previous chapters when Maurice materialized. "How do you like it so far?" he asked, sounding confident of hearing the right answer.

"Pretty good," I admitted. "Probably better than I could have done working on my own."

"Definitely better," Maurice corrected to his own satisfaction.

"But there *is* one little problem," said I.

He halted one leg in the act of swinging it across the other. "What problem do you *imagine* you see?"

"Seems to be getting dull."

"Dull!"

"Not dull, exactly. More like repetitive."

"Repetitive!"

"And not as much fun."

"Not. As. Much. Fun." Maurice repeated each word slowly and distinctly so that I might be able to correct anything that he had misheard.

"Here's the score, Maurice. So far, all the girls have been forced into early marriages, happy or unhappy, to keep them from entering the nearest convent. And the boys have been ridiculed, harassed, or threatened for following their vocations. I know parents aren't the most imaginative people in the world, but surely they can do better than this!"

Maurice had relaxed a little bit. "What you're saying is not that *I'm* dull, repetitive, and not as much fun, but that these saints' *lives* are dull, repetitive, and not as much fun. Is that correct?"

"Well . . . yeah."

"Thank goodness." The right leg was finally free to slide over the left one. "For a minute there, I was afraid I was losing my touch. You want something different?"

St. Martin of Tours

"Right."

"How about the father who drafted his son into the army?"

"That's different," I agreed as I picked up my pencil. "Who is it?"

"St. Martin of Tours."

"Patron of travel agents?" I suggested.

"Bishop of the city of Tours, in Gaul," Maurice corrected sternly, "and a staunch fighter of heresy. And, for a brief time, a soldier of Rome."

"St. Martin was born in the year 316 or 317 . . ."

"A saint lies about his age?"

"We don't have a record of his exact date of birth. Rather, *we* do, but *you* don't. He was born in Sabaria, in Lower Hungary, not far from the Austrian border. He didn't live there long though. When he was still a baby, his family moved to Pavia, Italy. His father, I should mention, was an officer in the Roman army."

"What was the Roman army up to at this time?"

"Fighting barbarians, mostly. That comes a little later. It was in Pavia that Martin went to school, and in Pavia that he discovered the Christain religion. His parents were fervent pagans, and they were none too pleased to learn that their son was hanging around the local chapel. They were even less pleased when he asked the local priest to accept him as a catechumen. And he *was* accepted, even though he was only ten years old at the time."

"What's a catechumen? An altar boy?"

"A non-Catholic who wants to learn more about the Church. After studying for several years and being found worthy, he may be baptized and permitted to become a Catholic."

"Several years? That's a long time."

"It wasn't always easy to join the Church. You couldn't just walk in and be baptized on the spot. You had to know what you believed, what the Church was all about. It was like entering a college. They wouldn't take just anybody. They wanted dedicated Christians. Not just Sunday Catholics, but Catholics for every day in the year."

"You've got that nostalgic ring in your voice again."

"Sorry." He wiped his eyes on his sleeve. "Where was I?"

"Martin just became a catechumen."

"Ah yes. His parents weren't happy about his new interest, but there wasn't much they could do about it. His father spent most of his time at the wars, and his mother decided to let him have his new hobby, hoping that he'd soon lose interest in it and go on to more, umm, natural things."

"Like killing barbarians?"

"That sort of thing, among others, yes. But the more Martin studied, the deeper his love for God grew. By the time he was twelve, his greatest wish was to go off into the desert to pray and meditate in solitude."

"Like John the Baptist."

"But he didn't get the chance. His spiritual adviser suggested that he wait until he was a little older, that he should stay at home and continue his studies. Martin obeyed."

"Smart kid."

"He was pretty smart, but he trusted people a bit too much when he was young. That spiritual adviser had cause to regret his advice a few years later.

"In 331 A.D., when Martin was about fifteen years old, the emperor issued an order commanding the sons of veteran officers and soldiers to take up weapons and join their fathers in glorious conquest. That was just the sort of command Martin's father had been waiting for. He had planned all along for his son to follow in his footsteps."

"Parents have a habit of doing that."

"Not only could he start Martin upon his preselected career, he could also take him far away from the influence of the accursed Church and turn his mind to "more serious" matters. And so Martin was taken from his home and friends and enrolled in the Roman army."

"That same year?"

"Yes."

"But Martin was only fifteen."

"The Roman army didn't ask questions about age. If a man could draw a sword or fling a spear, he was in. Younger boys than Martin were in the army."

"I guess he wasn't very happy about going."

"He didn't jump for joy, if that's what you mean. But he accepted the will of his parents as the will of God—"

"Another accepter."

"—and obeyed his father. The thing that grieved him most was having to abandon his lessons before he was baptized."

"He'd been studying for five years and *still* wasn't baptized?"

"He hadn't finished the course yet."

"In five years he could have gotten a college diploma and spent a year abroad."

"But that wasn't what he wanted. He wanted to be a Christian. Even more awful than that, he sometimes dreamed of becoming a priest."

"Horrors!"

*Martin was taken from his home and friends
and enrolled in the Roman army.*

"And horror would have come of it—if his father had ever found out. But Martin was smart enough to keep silent."

"Though not smart enough to stay out of the army."

"It all worked out in the end."

"*It* has a way of doing that."

"*God* has a way of doing that," Maurice corrected.

"So what was life like in the Roman army?"

"Not as terrible as your face would suggest. The Roman army was a pretty decent outfit. Cleanliness, order, discipline, and respect, both for self and for others, was the order of the day. I'm not saying that the soldiers were gentlemen in every respect, but on the whole the men were as pleasant as possible, considering that they were engaged in the business of war.

"Of course, Martin was somewhat better off than other new soldiers. As the son of an officer, he was entitled to a position in the cavalry, the army's elite corps, complete with rank and as many servants as he needed. He accepted only one, a boy about his age, whom we shall call Lucius, as his name escapes me at the moment."

"Which is more than Lucius ever did."

"He didn't *want* to escape, not after he got to know Martin. Martin didn't see Lucius as inferior in any way. He knew that they were equal in the sight of God. They often ate together and talked together. And Martin was not above doing for Lucius what Lucius was supposed to do for him."

"Lucius must have been amazed."

"He was. But he appreciated his good fortune. His devotion to Martin caused as much comment among the soldiers as Martin's devotion to the poor."

"The poor soldiers or the poor barbarians?"

"The poor wherever he could find them. But he hadn't found the barbarians yet. They come later. As a Roman soldier, Martin received a handsome allowance. He kept only what he needed for food and other daily expenses, using the rest to help those in need, whether soldiers or civilians. His tent door was always open to those who needed a friendly ear or good advice, not to mention good money."

"He must have been the most popular soldier on base."

"Not really. For each one who came to him for help and left calling him friend, there were two who laughed at him and called him fool, among other things."

"Are saints always called fools?"

"Almost always."

St. Martin of Tours

"That's comforting to know."

"There was one special act of mercy that benefitted Martin as well as the person helped. St. Sulpicius, his first biographer, recorded it, and I've heard it hundreds of times since.

"The army was on the march, looking for barbarians."

"Which barbarians?"

"Hang on, I'm getting to that. As the army came to the gates of Amiens, a small town in France, Martin met an almost naked man begging alms of the passing soldiers. The man wasn't old or sick, but he was quite destitute. It was snowy and cold, hardly a good season for wearing rags."

"There's a *good* season for wearing rags?"

"There are seasons when rags are more bearable. Martin, being Martin, immediately wanted to give him something. But he had already given away all his money, and his next pay packet was some days away. He had nothing left but the sword on his belt and the clothes on his back. So without hesitation he drew his sword . . ."

"And put the fellow out of his misery."

"Quite so."

"He didn't!"

"He did."

"He killed him?"

"No! He cut his own cloak in two and gave half of it to the poor man."

"Oh."

"The beggar could scarcely believe what he saw. Martin apologized for not having any money or food or other comfort to give him. In truth the fellow would have appreciated a coin or two, but he rejoiced in what Martin had left to give and thanked him for his gift.

"The response of his comrades in arms was equally divided between those who laughed at such generous foolishness and those who felt a little ashamed that they hadn't helped the beggar themselves. A few of them pressed coins into his hands as they pased."

"It was a great day for the beggar, eh?"

"*He* certainly thought so.

"The Roman army had to camp outdoors that night. Even the mighty bonfires they built didn't keep them warm. Martin, with half a cloak, was in the worst predicament. Lucius offered to lend him his own cloak, but Martin insisted that he use it himself. He had offered his own cloak willingly, and willingly he suffered the loss of it.

"During the long, cold night, Martin had a wonderful dream. He saw the Man he loved and longed to serve."

"Jesus Christ?"

"Lucky guess."

"Did he wake up?"

"No. He was too awestruck to wake up. Not only did he see Jesus, he saw Him wearing the half of his own cloak that he had given to the beggar.

"Jesus smiled at him, called him by name, and said, 'Martin, yet a catechumen, has clothed me with this garment.' Then the vision faded, the dream ended, and Martin woke up."

"Warm as toast, I bet."

"I can tell you that he didn't feel the cold.

"After the initial thrill wore off and Martin's thoughts were close to earth again, he suddenly remembered that he had never finished his Christian training. He had never been baptized. He decided to correct that situation as soon as possible.

"In the morning he told Lucius of his dream and what he intended to do about it. Lucius pledged his help but warned Martin that his father wasn't going to be happy about the idea."

What was Martin's father doing during all this almsgiving and cloak ripping and counseling stuff?"

"Hoping that it would soon go away. He couldn't object to it, exactly. He thought his son was being a good soldier—an exceptionally kind one, but a good one. He had no idea that Martin's faith had not faltered. He thought his plan was working out quite well."

"He must have flipped when Martin was baptized."

"He was not a happy man."

"Martin had served in the army for three years before that night at Amiens. He was therefore eighteen years old when he found a priest (which wasn't difficult in France) and became a member of the Church in water and in spirit. His servant followed his example."

"Is that a tear in your eye, Maurice?"

"I can't help it. I always cry at baptisms."

"I thought Martin couldn't be baptized because he hadn't finished his studies."

"He had *nearly* finished. As he was a soldier and obviously possessed a great love of God, the priest was inspired to bend the rules a little in his behalf."

"What did Martin's father do when he found out?"

"He was furious, but his anger cooled a little when he learned that Martin wasn't planning to leave the army. He wanted to; he wanted to head straight to the nearest monastery, but Lucius asked him to stay on.

St. Martin of Tours

He promised that if Martin would remain for another year or two, he would leave with him and join him in his work for God.

"So Martin stayed to please his father and his friend. But he wasn't the same conscientious soldier he had been before his dream. His thoughts were all on his future. Often he expressed his impatience. Why should he stay in the army when his life belonged to God? But Lucius kept him to his promise."

"Sounds like the days of suffering in silence are over."

"But he was still open to those people who came to him for help. Lucius kept his soldier's gear in inspection-passing order and covered up his negligences as best he could.

"*Now* we come to the barbarians."

"Hooray!"

"In about 335 or 336 A.D., the Franks, the Allemanni, and other assorted groups broke through the Roman boundaries around Gaul and wreaked a great deal of havoc. Cologne, Worms, Strassburg—a number of towns and small cities, were sacked, burnt, pillaged, and looted by these gentlemen."

"Weren't there any Roman troops nearby, Maurice? Gaul was part of the Roman Empire, wasn't it?"

"It was part of the frontier—much like the American West was not so long ago. Of course troops were stationed there. But the men were so scattered and few, so poor of provisions, arms, and strength that they could not stop the invaders. In fact they fled before them."

"The emperor isn't going to like that."

"He didn't. As soon as the news reached him, he charged into action."

"What did he do?"

"He—his name was Julian, by the way; you may have heard of him—ordered fresh troops into Gaul and took command of them himself. Martin's outfit was among them. Julian also saw to it that each man was given a donative."

"Is that a bribe?"

"Close. It's a sum of money over and above the weekly pay packet, given to encourage the men to fight well and to hint that there might be more goodies forthcoming if they did their duty."

"In other words, to the victor belong the spoils."

"Julian planned to give out these donatives himself as a further morale booster. Martin's camp was electrified when they heard of Julian's imminent arrival. Martin was excited, too, but for a different reason. He had decided that he wasn't going to stay in the army one moment longer than he had to. No matter what his father said, no matter what Lucius said, he knew the time was ripe to leave the army and enter the priesthood."

"Switching from being a soldier of the emperor to a soldier of Christ."

"Well put."

"I *am* a writer, you know."

"So you keep saying. When Martin learned about the donative, he knew he could not accept it. He didn't feel it was fair to take the money when he planned to leave the army as soon as possible. He would step forward when his turn came, but rather than accept the emperor's gift, he would request to be released from military service.

"When Martin told his plan to Lucius, Lucius instantly tried to talk him out of it."

"Smart kid."

"But Martin wouldn't listen to reason. He was determined to resign at that moment. A great battle lay ahead, and he did not want to risk shedding other men's blood, be they Romans or barbarians."

"Or risk having his own blood shed."

If looks could cut, the glare in Maurice's eyes would have left me in ribbons.

"What does that remark mean?"

"Wasn't Martin at least partially interested in preserving his own life," I suggested as tactfully as I could, "if only so that his life could be spent in the service of Christ rather than wasted on the field of battle?"

"You mean, was he chickening out? Choosing a convenient time to respond to God's will?"

"After all, Maurice, it does seem a little suspicious, a little too coincidental. But, of course, I could be wrong."

Maurice stared pensively over my head. After a moment's hard thought, he began, "Off the record . . . "

"No. *On* the record. My readers will want to know this."

"*On* the record"—he managed the transition smoothly—"there was a teensy bit of the self-preserving instinct in Martin's decision. He was pretty sure that God wouldn't let him be killed on the field of battle. On the other hand, a little insurance couldn't hurt."

"Ah-ha! A wavering of faith!"

"Temporary, I assure you."

"So he went to Julian."

"Yes. He came before the emperor with the rest of the men to receive the donative, but he didn't accept it. As he stood before Julian, he made a speech that went something like this:

St. Martin of Tours

Hitherto I have served you as a solider; let me now serve Christ. Give the bounty to these others who are going to fight, but I am a soldier of Christ and it is not lawful for me to fight.

"What a nervy kid!"

"That's almost exactly what Julian thought. Martin's father nearly went into shock. Lucius trembled in his hiding spot at the rear of the assembly. The troops stood stock still and waited to see what would happen next.

"After the understandable moment of shock had passed, Julian recovered his voice and his temper, both mighty and much feared. He accused Martin of cowardice, just as you did."

"I didn't *accuse* him," I protested. "I just *suggested*. And I didn't say 'cowardice.' I said 'self-preservation.' "

"But you were thinking *cowardice*."

"I . . ."

"Don't deny it. I saw you. And both you and Julian were wrong. To prove that he wasn't a coward, Martin offered to stand in front of the Roman army as the enemy advanced, with no weapon to use in his defense, no horse for escape. His exact words, as I recall them, were, 'In the name of the Lord Jesus, and protected not by helmet and buckler but by the sign of the cross, I will thrust myself into the thickest squadrons of the enemy without fear.'

"Now," said Maurice, after making the speech in the grandest manner possible, "do you know what happened next?"

I nodded. "He was given a Section Eight."

Up to that moment I had never seen an angel blink.

"A what?"

"A Section Eight."

"What on earth is a Section Eight?"

"It's a discharge for reason of insanity."

Maurice snorted his disgust. "He was not!"

"Discharged? Or insane?"

"Neither. Julian didn't accept madness as an excuse for not fighting barbarians. And Martin was not mad."

"He was mad with the madness of God."

"Spoken like a poet. However, that is not true insanity. True insanity is—well, never mind that now. You've gotten me off the track. Where were we?"

"Martin just made the speech about standing in front of the army."

"Ah yes. There was a moment of total silence after that stirring speech."

"Yeah, the men were mourning Martin's death before it came to pass."

"Julian seemed to be considering the idea. While Martin waited calmly for an answer, faithful Lucius trembled in the safety of the rear guard. He didn't know what was going to happen, but he privately vowed that if Julian should tell Martin to do this crazy thing, he would stand with him."

"What guts."

"I prefer the word *loyalty* myself."

"So Julian told him to try it and see what happens?"

"No. Julian ordered him into irons."

"Why?"

"For threatening to desert. There are no deserters in the Roman army."

"But he didn't threaten to desert!"

"Julian thought he did. And what the emperor thinks is law."

"He *should* have deserted."

"No. Martin couldn't slink away in the dead of night. He wasn't that kind of man."

"I know, Maurice. He was a saint."

"Martin's father nearly died of shame on the spot. When some time had passed and Julian's temper had cooled, he asked to see his son. But his request was refused, a wise decision as far as Martin's well-being was concerned. His father had recovered enough from his shame to want to kill him."

"Typical parent."

"Lucius lingered near the jail tent, trying to keep his master in good spirits. Martin used the solitude to meditate and pray, and didn't much mind the discomfort put upon him."

"So what happened when the barbarians attacked?"

"They didn't."

"They didn't?"

"That night a delegation from the barbarians arrived in the Roman camp and sued for peace."

"Some barbarians!"

"The barbarians had scouted the army. They knew its size and strength. They knew that Julian himself was there and that they could not possibly win. So they decided to surrender before they were sundered."

"The soldiers must have been greatly disappointed."

St. Martin of Tours

"There were more than a few of them who were also greatly relieved."

"That problem having been handled, Julian prepared to leave. But before he returned to his court, he was kind enough to set Martin free, not only from the emperor's jail but from his army as well."

"Free at last!"

"Free at last."

"And Lucius went with him?"

"And Lucius went with him."

"And Daddy had a fit."

"And Daddy had a fit," Maurice concurred, "but he couldn't go against the emperor."

"Martin and Lucius bade farewell to all their friends and comrades in arms and set out for Poitiers, where St. Hilary, then the bishop of that city, waited for them with open arms."

"And so Martin lived happily ever after, huh?"

"More or less. He went back home and converted his mother and several friends to the Christian faith—after he became a priest, that is—but his father refused even to consider the idea."

"Stubborn to the last."

"Romans like stubborness."

"So what's the moral here? What can we learn from St. Martin's life?"

"Perseverance pays," Maurice intoned. "Trust in God. Keep the faith. Need any more?"

"Three are enough for one saint. That's plenty of work for one day too. I'm getting writer's cramp."

"Very well. I'll come back tomorrow."

"Bring some milk and cookies with you."

"You bring the snacks. It's *your* planet."

ST. ALOYSIUS

"This is a surprise," Maurice said sincerely when he dropped in (or down, if you prefer) at the appointed time.

"How so?" I asked.

"Usually I find you eating cookies or reading magazines or shooting paper clips across the room. I hardly ever find you writing."

"I'm not actually writing. I'm spelling."

"Spelling what?"

"*Aloysius.* I always want to write A-l-o-y-i-s-u-s."

"You're improving," Maurice pointed out. "You used to write A-l-o-y-w-i-s-h-u-s."

"That was before sixth grade, when I had Sister Mary Aloysius for my teacher."

"And the minute you got into seventh grade, you forgot how to spell her chosen name. How quickly you mortal youths forget! Think you've refreshed your memory enough?"

I put my pencil down and stretched my fingers. "Twenty-five times should be sufficient."

"We'll soon see."

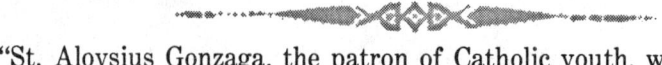

"St. Aloysius Gonzaga, the patron of Catholic youth, was born into a family of considerable wealth and power. His father was Ferdinand Gonzaga, prince of the Holy Roman Empire and marquis of Castiglione, close in blood and friendship to the duke of Mantua. Ferdinand had the excellent taste to fall in love with Martha Tana Santena, daughter of Tanus Santena, lord of Cherry, in Piedmont, Italy. She served as lady of honor to Isabel, wife of Philip II of Spain. The young marquis was also in service at the royal court. It was within this glittering circle that they met, fell in love, and were married."

St. Aloysius

"Fairy tales really happened."

"After their marriage, they asked Philip's permission to return to their homeland of Italy. He gave his consent and his blessing. As if that weren't enough, he declared the marquis to be chamberlain to his majesty and general of part of the army in Lombardy. For all of this, the newlyweds were grateful. But nothing gave them as much pleasure as their return to Ferdinand's old and Martha's new home, the castle Castiglione delle Stivieri in Lombardy. Here their first child, Aloysius, was born on March 9, 1568.

"From the very beginning, Ferdinand had determined that his son would be a soldier. When he was four years old, he gave Aloysius a fantastic birthday present: a set of miniature guns to play with."

"You mean toys?"

"No. They were real. But he *did* refrain from giving the boy ammunition."

"And, I suppose, Aloysius, as befits a future saint, despised such tools of violence and spent his time in prayer."

"He loved his birthday presents and played with them every chance he got."

"That's not very holy."

"How holy can you be at four years old?"

"I can think of some girls who were quite holy at four years old. But I'd forgotten that holiness is more difficult for boys."

Maurice's upper lip curled at my blatantly sexist remark. But I noticed that he didn't deny it.

"If Aloysius's mother was alarmed by her son's military interests—and she was—she was almost overcome by what he got for his fifth birthday. His father took him on a special trip to Casalmaggiore, where three thousand soldiers were in training for a Spanish expedition to Tunis."

"Every kid's birthday dream."

"Aloysius enjoyed himself. He got to march in the parades, lead platoons with a pike swung over his shoulder, and enjoy the attentions of the entire army, which is a pretty heady thing for a five-year-old—or anyone else for that matter."

"Sounds like he was there for more than a day."

"A couple of months."

"Beats school."

"He might have stayed longer if he hadn't gotten himself into trouble.

"Aloysius usually woke up before the rest of the camp. He liked to wander around in the chily gray dawn when there was no one around to

69

*Aloysius got his hands on a real gun
and some real ammunition.*

St. Aloysius

make him behave. On one of those mornings, he got his hands on a real gun and some real ammunition that some raw recruit had carelessly left lying around. He decided to see if this big gun worked like his toy guns at home.

"At the first shot, the entire camp woke up and scrambled out into the field, clutching the first weapons that came to hand and shivering in their underwear or less. They were not amused to find one small boy and one big gun at the heart of the attack."

"I *like* this kid."

"He was properly punished, though his father grinned a lot while he did it, and sent home to rejoin his mother and brother and the rest of his family. He didn't arrive empty-handed. He had presents for some, messages for all, and quite a few brand-new words he had picked up from the men in the ranks."

"Such as?"

"Do you expect to hear an angel use that kind of language?"

"Oh, *those* brand-new words."

"He didn't realize that there was anything naughty about them until his tutor told him. The tutor exaggerated the seriousness of the matter, telling the boy how blasphemous he was and how terrribly he was sinning.

"The scolding made a deep impression on Aloysius. He begged God's forgiveness for days, even cried on his knees. Throughout the rest of his life he never ceased to regret his sin—though it wasn't truly a sin, since he didn't realize what he was doing—and couldn't stand being near people who abused God's name."

"Why should he suffer so much guilt for something that really wasn't a sin?"

"His tutor treated it as though it had been a sin, and even his mother couldn't convince him otherwise.

"From this time on, Aloysius's devotion to God began to grow. When he was seven years old, he took up reciting the Office of Our Lady and the seven penitential psalms every day, on his knees, in addition to his regular prayers. He studied hard, helped others, and led an exemplary life—though you don't seem to approve of it."

"I'm sorry, Maurice. These superprayerful kids always make me feel queasy."

"That's envy."

"How do you know?"

"I know. While he was devoting himself to good works, he came down with ague and remained ill for almost two years."

"Oh. Sorry."

"What do you mean?"

"I queased too soon. If I had ague for eighteen months, I'd have prayed a lot too . . . I think. What's ague?"

"Ague is a fever accompanied by shivering spells. It features hot and cold flashes. Not very pleasant, especially not for a child. But Aloysius finally shook it.

"When Aloysius was eight years old, his father took him and his younger brother, Ridolfo, to the court of Francis of Medici, grand duke of Tuscany, and left them there to receive a suitably royal education. This was in Florence, by the way, in a court that has been described as a society that featured 'fraud, dagger, poison, and lust of the most hideous kind.' "

"In other words, all the nasty things an ambitious young prince needed to learn."

"One might say that.

"Aloysius did well in his formal studies, but he wasn't very interested in the subjects just mentioned. He cultivated strong habits of modesty. When he spoke to a woman, he kept his eyes on her shoes or the hem of her skirt, never daring to look at her face and risk being tempted to sin."

"At the age of *eight*? Come on!"

"He took the ideas of sin and temptation very seriously. I can think of some people who would do well to follow his example."

"Don't preach, please. Get on with the story."

"Feeling queasy again?"

"How long did the boys stay in Florence?"

"Until Aloysius was eleven, about three years. Then their father transferred Aloysius and Ridolfo to the care of Duke William Gonzaga, who lived in Mantua."

"Why the switch?"

"Gonzaga, who had just made their father the governor of Montserrat, extended the invitation, which he was glad to accept. There were also family ties to consider. Remember Aloysius's last name?"

"Gonzaga. Aha!"

"*Gonzaga* will do."

"By the time the two boys arrived in Mantua, Aloysius had resolved to let his brother take over the family business and to devote himself to spiritual matters. Exactly how he planned to do this, or what vocation he would choose, he wasn't sure.

"While at Mantua, Aloysius came down with kidney trouble."

"Back to the prayers again."

"He had never left them. He used his illness as a perfect excuse not to mingle in court life. Mantua wasn't as corrupt as Florence, but it wasn't entirely holy either. He divided his time between study and prayer. In addition to his school books, Aloysius studied Surius's *Lives of the Saints* and other devotional works."

"Was he confined to bed all this time?"

"No, no. He was able to get around and about, especially during the summer, when Ferdinand brought him and Ridolfo home to Castiglione to enjoy the holidays."

"I guess he had the chance for a little fun then, huh?"

"Indeed he did. It was while he was at home that he came upon a little book on meditation written by Father Canisius and a collection of letters written by Jesuit missionaries in the Indies. These two works fired him with ambition. His future was clear. He would become a Jesuit."

"Ahem. I thought we were going to talk about fun in the summertime."

"We are. One of the first things he did was set up a one-teacher school for the poor boys in Castiglione, where he patiently taught them their catechism."

"This is *fun*?"

"For Aloysius it was."

"But for the boys?"

"If they didn't enjoy it, they wouldn't have come."

"I guess you're right."

"In 1580, when Aloysius was twelve, Cardinal Charles Borromeo, the future saint, came to Brescia, not far from Castiglione, to preach and to seek out any young lads in the area who might have religious vocations. As he refused to lodge with anyone but his fellow clergymen and, thus, wouldn't come near the homes of royalty, Aloysius went to Brescia to meet him and receive his blessing. Cardinal Borromeo was impressed by his knowledge and piety but amazed to discover that a boy of such strong faith had yet to make his First Holy Communion."

"Are you kidding?"

"Do I look as if I'm kidding?"

"But he was twelve years old!"

"But this was a long time ago. It wasn't until this century that communion for children was encouraged.

"Aloysius, happy to carry out his mentor's order, discovered that this sacrament brought him even closer to God.

"Shortly after this incident, the Gonzaga family moved to Casale, in northwest Italy, where Ferdinand's government was in residence.

Aloysius soon discovered the homes of the Capuchins and Barnabites and spent as much time in those sanctified places as he could.

"In 1581 . . ."

"Gads."

"What is it now?"

"Didn't his father ever hold a steady job?"

"He had to go where he was sent."

"But so often? I don't see how you can keep track of all these moves."

"Superhuman intelligence," Maurice said snidely.

"Not to be confused with the notes scribbled on your sleeve."

Maurice thrust his left arm out of sight. "In 1581, Ferdinand was sent to attend Empress Mary of Austria, wife to Maximilian II and sister to Philip II, as she traveled from Bohemia to Spain. The whole family got to go with him. Aloysius and his brother were appointed to serve as pages to King Philip's son, James. Aloysius was then thirteen years old.

"Aloysius chose this time to tell his parents what he had decided to do with his life: to give up his future title and become a Jesuit. His mother, a devout woman herself, rejoiced. His father threatened to flog him."

"Bit extreme, wasn't he?"

"You'll have to forgive him. He wasn't quite himself. He didn't think that his oldest son was so much responding to a call from God as attempting to shame his father into giving up his one great vice: gambling. Aloysius had made no secret of how offensive he had found this habit, not so much because his father rarely won—in fact, he once lost six hundred crowns in one night—as because of the injury done to God, who might have had better plans for the money."

"So Ferdinand flogged him?"

"No, he didn't. But he refused to give his consent for a long time. Finally, his friends persuaded him to change his mind."

"Why did Aloysius need his consent so soon?"

"He didn't, really. But he felt better about having it. Now he could plan for the future with a clear conscience. Or so he thought.

"Prince James died in 1582, which set the two Gonzaga boys free of their pageship. After touring Spain for a couple of years, they headed home in 1584. Aloysius was sorry about the young man's death, but he couldn't help rejoicing in his freedom. He planned to enter the nearest Jesuit seminary as soon as possible. Little did he suspect the surprise waiting for him at home."

"The flogging?"

"Would you be brokenhearted if I told you there wasn't going to be any flogging?"

St. Aloysius

"No. Just disappointed."

"*Why?*"

"Just thinking what a wonderful opportunity it would be for Aloysius to offer up his suffering to God."

"You'd like to see him get whopped, wouldn't you?"

"Who? Me?"

"The usual reaction of the impious to the pious."

"Hey! Watch who you'e calling impious, you . . ."

"I'll end your suspense. Aloysius *was* flogged. But not physically. Verbally. His father, who had retracted his consent, had assembled a crowd of relatives, churchmen, laymen, and the duke of Mantua himself to urge his firstborn son to come to his senses."

"In other words, away from his priesthood and to the life of a future marquis."

"That was the idea.

"Aloysius found himself severely outnumbered, but he faced them all with the courage a person finds when he knows that what he's doing is right. He met arguments, promises, and threats with equal aplomb. When he managed to win a few enemies over to his side, his father called the encounter session off."

"Gave up?"

"Hadn't yet begun to fight. He let Aloysius remain peacefully at home for a few days, then sent him on a trip to pay his respects to all the rulers of northern Italy. He reasoned that Aloysius might change his mind when he rediscovered the high life of the Italian courts.

"Aloysius saw everything he had seen before, and more. When he came home again, he was more determined than ever to become a priest."

"He must have seen more bad than good."

"The bad was easier to find. He was firmly convinced of the truth of Jesus' words, 'You cannot give yourself to God and money.'"

"Just a minute. I want to write that down."

"When the grand tour failed, Ferdinand buried his son under an avalanche of secular duties: paperwork, supervision of peasants—all the things he should have been doing himself. Needless to say, that didn't work either. Aloysius did the work, and did it well, but his heart wasn't in it."

"Saints aren't, or shouldn't be, bureaucrats."

"Say, rather, that a bureaucrat can be a saint but a saint is rarely a bureaucrat.

"Since both honey and vinegar had failed, Ferdinand saw that he had no choice but to retract his retraction. He went so far as to recommend Aloysius to Claudius Aquaviva, the general of the Society of Jesus, who cordially accepted him and decided he should serve his novitiate in Rome.

"That was not what Ferdinand had planned. He wanted Aloysius close by so that he could continue to argue with him and attempt to shake him from his faith. When Claudius refused to transfer Aloysius to another seminary, Ferdinand recaptured his son and kept him prisoner for nine months."

"Maurice, tell the truth: Wasn't Aloysius, future saint though he was, getting fed up with all this monkey business?"

"Definitely. But he hung on to his plan, his dream. He never gave up. And, eventually, as you may have have guessed, his father did. As always, patience and persistence triumph over adversity."

"Another quotable quote."

"With great reluctance and sorrow, Ferdinand gave his final consent."

"And Aloysius fled to Rome before he could change his mind again."

"No. He stayed at home, carefully avoiding his heartbroken father—not because he feared him but because he didn't want to cause him fresh grief—until the papers arrived that officially transferred the marquisate from himself to Ridolfo. That was in November of 1585. Then he took leave of his brooding father, his loving mother, his gleeful brother, and a host of family and friends, and proceeded in peace to the Holy City."

"Where, I suppose, he did much good and lived a singularly holy life."

"Correct. He died during the great distemper epidemic of 1591 at the age of twenty-three."

"The good die young."

"But not alone," Maurice said, with his most knowing smile. ◇

ST. ROSE OF VITERBO

"All rested from yesterday's exertions?" Maurice inquired sweetly.
"I think I'm good for about six pages."
"Who's next on your list?"
"St. Rose of Viterbo."
"And you accuse *me* of hunting up obscure saints!"
"Don't you know her, Maurice?"
"Of course I know her. I'm merely surprised that *you* do."
"I've done a little research, you know."
"As little as possible, I'm sure."
"Okay, Guardian Angel, let's hear how much *you've* done."
"With pleasure."

"The Emperor Frederick II and Pope Gregory IX did not get along well together. In fact, the Pope found it necessary to excommunicate Frederick. Twice. Frederick, in turn, found it necessary to invade the Papal States and wrest them from Gregory's control. He had to prove that no man on earth had power over him. In 1240, he seized Viterbo, a small village in the region of Italy known as the Romagna. His troops settled in for a good long stay.

"Five years earlier, in 1235, Rose had been born. Her family was not wealthy; in fact, they were nearer to poverty. But her life was pleasant enough, even when the emperor's troops—the Ghibellines, they were called—invaded and took over the town. Rose was a pleasant little girl, one of the favorite children of the neighborhood. She was liked by parents and peers, even if she *was* rather God-oriented."

"Figures."

"When Rose was eight years old, she came down with a serious illness. While she lay sick and feverish in bed, we are told that she was favored by a visit from the Blessed Virgin Mary. Our Lady told her that someday she would wear the Franciscan habit but that she would always live at home rather than enter a convent.

"When Rose recovered, she took a greater interest in spiritual matters than before. She meditated on the passion and death of Christ and on the irreverence and ingratitude of the sinners He had come to save. She also became more aware of Frederick's military government and its oppression of the Church and its people. Thus, when, at the age of twelve, she started to preach in the streets, she mixed her message of repentance with fiery words against the Ghibelline garrison. In the same breath, she urged the curious crowds to abandon their sins and to overthrow the enemy."

"That's the kind of talk that can get a kid in trouble. That is, if anyone took her seriously."

"Not too many people did at first. But when miracles and rumors of miracles began to happen around her, the crowds grew both in numbers and in faith. Soon they took to surrounding her house and begging for her to come out to speak to them and heal them.

"Her parents were terrified by these goings-on. Her father threatened her with a solid beating if she set foot outside the door again until all this fuss had blown over. Rose replied: 'If Jesus could be beaten for me, I can be beaten for Him. I do what He has told me to do, and I must not disobey Him.'"

"Spunky kid."

"Insolent, some would say. But her father couldn't argue her point."

"So he didn't beat her."

"No. But he kept her locked up in the house until their parish priest urged him to let her go. Even with her revolutionary message, she was doing more good than harm.

"Rose preached for the next two years. She brought many fallen-away Catholics back to the practice of their faith, but she was unable to convince her fellow townsmen to rise up against the invaders. However, Rose's appeal did not fall on totally deaf ears. The emperor's men were listening intently to everything she had to say. When they had heard enough, they sent a message to the podesta (a mayor, of sorts) of Viterbo requesting that the little girl be put to death on the grounds that she was a traitor and a danger to the state. She insisted on stirring up the people and demanding revolution.

"The podesta was a just and noble man who would never commit such a cowardly deed. He was also afraid of the wrath of the people, who acclaimed Rose as a heroine and saint. But he couldn't completely ignore the rulers of Viterbo either, not without losing his own life. He changed her fate from death to banishment."

"Bad enough."

"Not so bad that her parents couldn't go with her. The three of them went to Soriano, which wasn't too far away. Their many friends mourned their leaving, and the tide of public opinion slowly shifted against all the benefits Emperor Ferderick's rule had to offer.

"In 1250—about a year after she was forced to leave her home—Rose foretold Frederick's death. I don't know if he heard about her prediction, but he did die within the month. The Pope's men regained control of Viterbo shortly thereafter, and Rose and her family were allowed to return.

"After the fuss and excitement had died down, Rose applied for admittance to the convent of St. Mary of the Roses. The nuns turned her down, not because they didn't think she was holy enough, but because she had no dowry."

"I thought dowries came with weddings."

"In those days, they also came with convents. When a young lady became a nun, a 'bride of Christ,' she was expected to present her chosen convent with a suitable gift of money from her parents or herself. Not all convents enforced this custom, just the wealthy ones, ones like St. Mary of the Roses.

"Rose took this rebuff with her usual grace. As I recall, her parting words to the mother superior were, 'Very well, you will not have me now, but perhaps you will be more willing when I am dead.'"

"She wanted in, dead or alive?"

"She wanted the sisterhood very much."

"But the Blessed Virgin told her that she wouldn't enter a convent, that she would always live at home."

"I know."

"Why put her words to the test?"

"You'll have to ask Rose herself that question. But I will say that I have noticed in humans that they most want what they cannot have. If Rose remembered Our Lady's words—and I am sure she did—she knew she wouldn't succeed. Maybe she had to prove it to herself, or to her family. After her first visit to the convent, she didn't go back again.

"Rose might have been willing to give up, but her parish priest was not. When he heard that she had been rejected, he offered her the use of a chapel near the convent. There was a small house attached to it where Rose and some of her friends could live. Rose accepted his kind offer. The little group adopted Franciscan dress and joyfully began to live a holy and private life.

"But the peace and contentment Rose and her friends found in their tiny convent was short-lived. The nuns of St. Mary of the Roses didn't care to have this poor community so close to them, upstaging them, as it were. They fired off a letter to Pope Innocent IV, requesting that this pseudo-nunnery be closed on the grounds that the older group, because of its size, tenure, and wealth, had the right to be the only convent in town. The Pope agreed with them. The parish priest had no choice but to agree with the Pope.

"Rose obediently returned to her home. She fulfilled the rest of Our Lady's prophecy by staying there, continuing her good works and devotions until she died on March 2, 1252. She was seventeen years old."

"Good story, Maurice. After she died, I suppose the nuns were sorry they had treated her so snobbishly and asked that she be buried in their church."

"Wrong. Rose was buried in the church of Santa Maria-in-Podio. It wasn't until September of 1258 that she was moved to the convent church."

"Why was she moved?"

"I'm not sure," Maurice admitted. "Perhaps, as you said, the nuns saw the error of their ways. Maybe a miracle or two persuaded them. Or maybe the popular clamor of Rose's sainthood got to them. In any case, her words came true."

St. Rose of Viterbo

"Kind of a hollow victory. After you die, what does it matter what happens to you? To your *body*, I mean," I added hastily, before Maurice could reprimand me.

"It may not matter to you, but it may matter to the people who love you. And a great many people loved Rose."

"Excluding the good sisters of St. Mary of the Roses."

"That changed, too, in time."

"When it was too late for Rose."

"But not too late for them."

I don't mind Maurice's mysterious statements half as much as I mind the way he vanishes immediately after he makes them. ◈

ST. WENCESLAUS

"Where have you been?" Maurice demanded before I even got near my desk.

"You're my guardian angel. You should know where I was."

"You're late," he said, his wings all aflutter, "fifteen minutes late."

"You know why I'm late."

"My time is too important to be wasted by dillydallying mortals," Maurice sniffed.

"You *do* know where I was, don't you?"

"I certainly do. You were positively basking in food. A cheeseburger and a chocolate shake for lunch! And only yesterday you practically swore you were going on a strict diet."

"I didn't have french fries," I said, rather meekly.

"Omission doesn't excuse commission," said Maurice, relenting only a little.

"Didn't you say we were already late?"

"Seventeen minutes late now," Maurice said—without looking at my alarm clock. I didn't bother to look either. I knew he was right.

"We can get started, Guardian Dear, as soon as you get out of my chair."

He slid up and stretched out on his favorite patch of air, directly over my desk, a look of impatient suffering on his face. I expected to get a flood of grace from sitting in an angel's place. All I got was a warm, comfortable sensation and a hint of frankincense and myrrh.

"It's beginning to smell a lot like Christmas," I observed.

"That's a saint cue if I ever heard one."

"What do you mean, Maurice?"

"When you think of Christmas, who comes to mind?—excluding members of the holy family and their friends and relations and all three kings."

I thought back over my favorite carols. "A shepherd watching flocks by night?"

"No."

"A merry gentleman?"

"No."

"A master in the hall?"

"No. Remember the one you sing when you're walking home from the bus stop in the snow when you think no one can hear you?"

" 'Good King Wenceslaus'?"

"Correct."

"Great, Maurice! I feel like a Christmas story."

"I'm afraid it's not a Christmas story. But you'll like it anyway."

"Our tale begins in Bohemia, in Eastern Europe, in the long-ago tenth century, when civilization was barely making a dent in the wild and savage world. In the early 900s, Borivoy, the ruler of Bohemia, and his wife, Ludmilla, now known as a saint, were baptized into the Church. Duke Borivoy's subjects did not follow their leader. Some of them did, but most of them, including many powerful Czech families, remained antagonistic to the new religion, and to the new government as well.

"In the year 915, Borivoy, Bohemia's first Christian duke, died and was succeeded by his son, who was known as Duke Ratislav. He brought with him his wife, Drahomira, and their two sons, Wenceslaus and Boleslaus. Though Drahomira had been baptized, she was still practically a pagan.

"The widowed Ludmilla developed a special affection for her grandson Wenceslaus. In him she saw something of her own sensitivity and intelligence. Ludmilla persuaded Ratislav, her son, to allow her to take charge of the boy's education."

"I'm sure Drahomira was crazy about *that* idea."

"There wasn't much the boy's mother could do about it. Ratislav had made up his mind, and she had to let Wenceslaus go and live with his grandmother. But then she gave all her fierce devotion to her younger son, Boleslaus. Like his mother, Boleslaus had no interest in religion."

"Like her," I added, "he was easily corrupted."

"You're getting ahead of me. Besides, I'm not sure *corrupt* is the right word. I'm sure she meant well."

"People who mean well cause more trouble than all the villains in the world."

"Another sweeping statement impossible to prove by earthly means.

"Between Ludmilla and her chaplain, a priest who had been a personal disciple of St. Methodius, Wencelaus received a thorough schooling. Within a few years, he had mastered both Latin and Slavonic, neither of them an easy language, and had earned a sterling reputation as a scholar and a Christian, neither of them a healthy thing to be at that time and place. He was ready to move on to college at Budech when his father was killed by Magyars.

"By rights, the throne should have gone to Wenceslaus, as he was the oldest son. But his mother took over before he learned that his father was dead. I should note that she wasn't acting alone. She had been persuaded by the pagan nobility to put in the kind of government that would eventually wipe out Christianity and return the pagans to power."

"Didn't she feel guilty about denying her son his royal rights?"

"She did. But the crafty nobles, playing on her jealousy of Ludmilla, convinced her that Wenceslaus would be happier as a priest than as a king."

"Most of the saints we've seen *would* be happier that way."

"But not Wenceslaus. The idea occurred to him, but only as a passing fancy.

"When Ludmilla discovered what was happening, she urged Wenceslaus to hurry home and challenge his mother before she could get a firm grip on the government. He was the rightful duke. He should have no trouble rallying the people to his cause. The young man—he was seventeen or eighteen now—obeyed his grandmother at once.

"After he was gone, two nobles—allies of Drahomira—broke into the castle and strangled Ludmilla. They thought that Wenceslaus could not become duke without his grandmother's powerful support.

"But they were wrong. Wenceslaus had more friends than the pagan nobles knew. They invaded the royal palace, drove the terrified Drahomira and her supporters into the street, and proclaimed young Wenceslaus ruler of Bohemia.

"Wenceslaus laid down his law at once. He announced that he would uphold the laws of God and Church, punish murder severely, and try to govern his people with justice and mercy. To prove the latter promise, he welcomed his mother back to court and forgave her for her disloyalty. She never opposed him again."

"That's a wise mother."

"Despite his tender years, Wenceslaus proved to be a good duke. He established friendly relations with neighboring Germany and kept his country from being torn apart from within and without by acknowledging King Henry I as his overlord and the legitimate successor of the incomparable Emperor Charlemagne. In his own realm, he cracked down on the nobles who oppressed peasants—and everyone else they could annoy. He also performed many good deeds himself, usually at night and in secret. Hence the inspiration for your favorite Christmas carol.

"While his motives were good and reforms were needed, Wenceslaus offended a lot of powerful people. Even so, his reign might have lasted longer than it did—about seven years—if he hadn't made an unforgivable error."

"Let me guess. He stripped the nobles of their titles?"

"No."

"Oh, I know. He forced them to become Christians?"

"No."

"What, then?"

"He married a lovely young lady and fathered a son."

"What's so terrible about that?"

"The birth of a son knocked Boleslaus, his brother, out of the royal running. Unless some fatal accident were to befall Wenceslaus or the baby, Boleslaus would never be duke. He resolved to correct that situation and turned to the pagan nobles for help.

"In September of 929, Boleslaus extended a cordial invitation to his big brother to accompany him to Stara Boleslav to celebrate the feast of Cosmos and Damian, its patron saints. The unsuspecting duke agreed to go.

"On the eve of the festival, someone warned Wencelaus that his life was in danger, but he refused to take the report seriously.

"Early the next morning, as he was on his way to Mass, Wenceslaus met his brother in front of the cathedral doors. He thanked him for his hospitality. Boleslaus smiled and struck him.

"As the two brothers fought, they were surrounded by the young duke's enemies, who killed him. His last words were: 'Brother, may God forgive you.' He was twenty-two years old.

"Wenceslaus was instantly acclaimed as a martyr. Sainthood came soon after.

"So we see," Maurice concluded, "that it is not only parents who can give you problems. Brothers—or sisters—can bother you too."

"*I* could have told you that." ◆

ST. CATHERINE OF SIENA

"Do you realize, Maurice, that this is our last saint?"

"So soon?"

"Do I detect a note of sarcasm in your voice?"

"I seem to have been telling you stories for the past twelve years."

"It hasn't even been twelve days. And if you think your presence has been a total joy . . ."

"Shouldn't we strive to end this book on a friendly note?"

"You started it, Maurice, I didn't."

"I'm finishing it now. Shall we begin?"

"Fine with me. Tell me about St. Catherine of Siena."

Maurice's lips turned upward in what could almost be described as a devilish grin. "I *thought* you'd sympathize with her."

"Why?"

"You know the answer to that as well as I do. But in case your readers don't, allow me to proceed."

"Catherine was born in Siena, in what is now central Italy, in 1347. Her father was James Benincasa, a dyer and a pious man. Her mother was Lapa, an equally pious woman who developed a special affection for this particular daughter."

"Because she was the youngest?"

"No."

"Because she was the oldest?"

"No."

"Then why?"

"Because she was the twenty-fourth of the twenty-five children of that household. And because she was one of the prettiest, brightest children in the city. Her family and friends used to call her Euphrosyna."

"What in the world did the kid do to deserve to be called *that*?"

"They meant it as a compliment. But please don't ask me what it means. I'm not up on my Greek."

"In addition to her accomplishments in physical and mental realms, Catherine developed a strong interest in the spiritual kingdom. When she was still quite small, she imitated many saints before her by retiring to a solitary place a little way out of Siena to pray and meditate. She didn't stay too long—"

"Of course not. She had to be inside before dark."

"—but the experience left her with a deep longing for privacy. She turned one of the closets in her room into a little prayer chamber. She spent hours in there in communion with God, in perfect happiness."

"Gee, Maurice, is that one of the reasons you think I sympathize with her?"

"I'll grant you your longing for privacy, but I haven't seen you spending hours in communion with God lately."

"Just wait till I get this book finished."

"Sometime during these peaceful growing-up years, Catherine made a private vow to God that she would remain celibate. But since her parents didn't know about Catherine's vow, they had their eye out for eligible young men for her, normally a wise idea for parents who have a houseful of daughters.

"By the time Catherine turned twelve, her parents were all set to engage her to some fortunate young man."

"How come everything happens to you when you're twelve?"

"Just one of those happening ages, I guess. When her mother and father joyfully told Catherine of her forthcoming betrothal, her reaction wasn't at all what they thought it would be. She begged them to forget the idea, to let her live singly in the world. Her parents refused even to consider such a ridiculous notion. After fighting a good fight, Catherine gave up on changing their minds and retired to her room to pray.

"While she was gone, her parents held a war council. The time had come to 'do something about Catherine.' She was far too religious and far too private a person to live the life of a wife and mother. For her own good, she would have to be corrected and disciplined, no matter how much it hurt."

"Her or them?"

"Both."

"That's what they always say."

"The first thing they did was to take apart her prayer chamber. They carted out her holy pictures and books and turned her sanctuary into a regular closet again."

"Barbarians," I muttered softly, but Maurice chose to ignore my remark.

"They found excuses," he continued, "to interrupt her prayers and readings. At first they made her do little things, such as tending to the younger children or setting the table for supper. But when she remained sweet, good-tempered—and obstinate—they began to crack down hard."

"*Here* we go!"

"In no time at all, Catherine turned into the all-around slave of the household. She had to dust the furniture, wash the floors, cook the three daily meals, weed the gardens, keep the kitchen clean—the forever impossible task—and be at the beck and call of the entire family at any hour of the day or night. Name any disagreeable task, the chore you hate more than geometry class, and chances are that Catherine was made to do it."

"*This* is where I really sympathize."

"You and every child in America. But, unlike you and every child in America, Catherine did everything with a smile. No matter what names her sisters called her—and they called her quite a few—no matter how contemptuously her parents treated her, no matter how cracked and sore her hands became or how tired and hungry she was, Catherine kept her spirits up and her smile steady, always ready to be of service."

"How could she do it?"

"She had her faith to keep her warm. If God chose to send her this trial, He would also send her the strength to endure and even overcome it. Besides, loading Catherine with household work was keeping both her parents and herself too busy even to think about marriage."

"But there must have been times when she thought of giving in."

"Not totally. Her sisters pointed out that all she had to do to free herself was to apologize to her mother and father and consent to be married. She never went that far; but once, when the last of her dresses looked more like a dustcloth than the dustcloths did, she let them persuade her to dress a little more elegantly, in a gown borrowed from one of her sisters. When she came down to fix breakfast looking more like a daughter than a drudge, her parents thought the change was for the better—in their favor, that is—and lightened her work load accordingly. Before the end of the day, though, Catherine was ashamed of herself for weakening. She threw off the gaudy clothes and pulled on her filthy work dress. The next day, it was back to heavy labor."

"How long did this go on?"

"A long time. Catherine seems to have inherited her stubbornness from her parents. Unfortunately, it required the death of her older sister Bonaventura to end the struggle.

"Death makes life seem unworthy of petty feuds or grudge matches. In their grief, James and Lapa were able to swallow their pride and set Catherine free. She would be permitted to marry or not to marry, as she pleased. She could even have her prayer chamber back.

"Catherine accepted their apologies and begged them to accept her own. She would never have disobeyed them if she hadn't felt God was calling her in another direction. She hoped they understood that now.

"Catherine spent the next five years at home. Since she was free of more than her share of household work, she was able to help those less fortunate in the outside world. She visited people in prisons and people in sickbeds, donated her allowance to the poor, appeared wherever a smiling face and a light touch were needed. When she was eighteen, she was welcomed into the Order of St. Dominic as a Sister of Penitence and extended her ministry to wider spheres."

"An inspiring story."

"Do you see the moral?"

"Sure. 'Hang in there.'"

"I was thinking more along the lines of 'Housework won't kill you.'"

"I like mine better."

"I can tell," Maurice said, casting a disdainful look at my room.

AFTERWORD

I didn't see Maurice again until I'd finished all the note deciphering and rewriting and proofreading and typing—in other words, not until all the real work was done. I had just finished looking over the entire book when he chose to appear.

"How'd we do?" he asked cheerfully.

"Looks good to me," I said, "but I don't know if the editor will like it or not."

"*I* know," Maurice said with a smug smile.

"Well?"

"I can't tell you. I don't want to kill the suspense."

"Either the suspense dies or you do."

"Nonsense. You can't kill an angel."

"Has anyone ever tried?"

"You're in a violent frame of mind," Maurice complained as he discretely began to leave. "I thought you'd be grateful for all the help I gave you."

"Grateful? For the way you keep pushing and prodding me? For the way you got off a load of jokes and sarcasm at my expense? For abandoning me to do all the hard stuff on my own while you were off, Heaven knows where?"

"Are you finished?"

"No."

"Well?"

"Thank you."

Maurice grinned. "You're welcome."

Maurice's grin lasted a long time after he'd gone.

Just like the Cheshire cat.

In more ways than one. ◆